Techno-Vernacular Creativity and Innovation

Techno-Vernacular Creativity and Innovation

Culturally Relevant Making Inside and Outside
of the Classroom

Nettrice R. Gaskins

foreword by Leah Buechley
afterword by Ruha Benjamin

The MIT Press

Cambridge, Massachusetts | London, England

The MIT Press would like to thank the anonymous peer reviewers who provided comments on drafts of this book. The generous work of academic experts is essential for establishing the authority and quality of our publications. We acknowledge with gratitude the contributions of these otherwise uncredited readers.

This book was set in Stone Serif and Stone Sans by Westchester Publishing Services. Printed and bound in the United States of America.

Library of Congress Cataloging-in-Publication Data

Names: Gaskins, Nettrice R., author. | Buechley, Leah, author of foreword. |
    Benjamin, Ruha, author of afterword
Title: Techno-vernacular creativity and innovation : culturally relevant making
    inside and outside of the classroom / Nettrice R. Gaskins ; foreword by
    Leah Buechley; afterword by Ruha Benjamin.
Description: Cambridge, Massachusetts ; London, England : The MIT Press, 2021. |
    Includes bibliographical references and index.
Identifiers: LCCN 2020041263 | ISBN 9780262542661 (paperback)
Subjects: LCSH: Maker movement in education. | Culturally relevant pedagogy.
Classification: LCC LB1029.M35 G37 2020 | DDC 371.33--dc23
LC record available at https://lccn.loc.gov/2020041263

10 9 8 7 6 5 4 3 2 1

For my mother and the brave ones who came before her.

Contents

IV TVC and Culturally Relevant Making

Foreword

Leah Buechley

When I first saw Nettrice Gaskins's artwork, it took my breath away. I was especially dazzled by her series of algorithmically generated portraits. They are reminiscent of Chuck Close's paintings but less static—full of movement, vibrance, and blunt cultural weight. In them, iconic images of figures like Ella Fitzgerald, Marvin Gaye, and Colin Kaepernick have been remixed into swirling fields of color to communicate something new, alive, and urgent. These works, a collaboration between Gaskins and a machine learning algorithm, blend a lush and distinctive visual style with technical mastery and a quiet but sharp social-technical critique. They are, quite simply, stunning.

The power of Gaskins's work is also a painful reminder of the rarity of African American new media artists. Her images leave you with a feeling of excitement and also a stinging sense of absence. They are so unusual, so distinctive, that they make you wonder why you have never seen anything like them before. Her work makes it clear that there is so much creative territory that has not yet been explored. There are so many perspectives that have not yet been expressed or examined with computational media. There is so much yet to be done, so much yet to be seen.

Gaskins's work with young people is equally unique and impressive. Her carefully designed classes help diverse young people make connections between their cultural heritage and STEM (science, technology, engineering, and mathematics). She introduces programming and STEM in expressive and relevant contexts to youth who rarely get the opportunity to incorporate their identity into schoolwork. She appropriately honors history, culture, and the arts as much as STEM. Her educational efforts are broadening our conception of what "maker education" can be and, more importantly, whose work is seen and valued by the maker movement and traditional educational institutions.

In this book, Gaskins presents the theoretical framework that has grown out of her integrated scholarly, artistic, and educational career. It distills her working practices, experiences, and perspective into an inspiring and useful guide for researchers and practitioners. It provides an excellent overview of scholarship in culturally relevant educational practices, a clear structure to help educators recognize and value different cultural traditions, and a series of thought-provoking anecdotes that will be concretely useful to fellow artists and educators. There is so much to learn from her!

I hope that this volume can help those of us who wield power and influence in mainstream art, technology, and education circles to broaden the culture of STEM and STEAM (science, technology, engineering, art, and mathematics) so that new, transformative voices have the space and support they need to grow. And I hope that it will help us simply see and celebrate some of the vast creative territories that we haven't noticed before.

Acknowledgments

I dedicate this book to my late mother, Sharon Lee Gaskins, who, along with two other students, was the first to integrate Centre College in Danville, Kentucky, in 1964. When I was growing up, she was the only Black woman I knew who made a living as a computer programmer. Although I surely would not have believed it if someone told me then, I would one day learn computer programming as an undergraduate art student at Pratt Institute. My mother loved that I was an artist, and she recognized that I had other interests besides art. On my Christmas list in the third grade was a chemistry set and rock polishing kit. Writing this book reminded me of why I've been hopping around from discipline to discipline for such a long time. However, I have been and will always be the artist my mother wanted me to be and what I always wanted for myself.

This book would not have been possible without the encouragement and support of my teachers over the years. My high school art teacher, Susan Sidebottom, introduced me to computer graphics at a time when I had no interest in computers. I'm still not entirely sure why Mrs. Sidebottom decided to set up a computer lab and teach her students how to make art on computers. We're still friends, so maybe one day I will ask her. A host of people encouraged me to stay the course, including my grandmother Virginia Gill, Judyie and Shahid Al-Bilali (my early artist-mentors), my sister Tamboura, Audrey Bennett, Sheri Davis, Ron Eglash, Bettina Love, Nancy Nersessian, Celia Pearce, Juan A. Ramírez, and Jacqueline Royster. Without my book editors, Susan Buckley and Ronnie Lipton, this book would not have been completed. I thank both of them for their time, consideration, and encouragement. I'm also thankful for the commentary by Leah Buechley and Ruha Benjamin in this book.

It was Hank Shocklee who triggered the "Aha!" moment when I realized there was a connection between hip-hop music production and maker culture. It was my love of hip-hop culture, specifically graffiti art, that led to my discovery that artists were being intentional about using or referring to STEAM (science, technology, engineering, art and mathematics) concepts in their work. Many of these artists reflect the communities of the students I've taught, especially from African American, Latino/a, and Indigenous groups. Support from the National Science Foundation and the Georgia Institute of Technology in 2014 helped me create a workshop to bring together artists, learning scientists, educators, and other experts to explore and discuss methods for increasing participation of underrepresented ethnic groups in STEM through cultural art and design and digital media.

I'm grateful to the NSF workshop participants whose art has inspired me over the years, including Xenobia Bailey, James Eugene, L'Merchie Frazier, John Jennings, Michi Meko, my former student Destiny Palmer, Will Wilson, and Vanessa Ramos-Velasquez. These amazing artists were willing and able to spend two-plus days with STEM experts to find common language and brainstorm ideas. They recommended that I set up and run a STEAM lab, which I did for three years at Boston Arts Academy after completing my doctoral work.

Also, I am grateful to Libby Rodriguez, whose master's thesis created the Afrofuturism culturally situated design tools that I used to teach students. The artist Saya Woolfalk was also instrumental in the development of the software. Without Barrington Edwards, a former BAA visual arts teacher, I would not have had the opportunity to run a STEAM lab in an arts high school. Thanks to Christi Wilkins, Susan Klimczak, and Agnes Chavez, I was able to work with youth in Long Beach, California, Boston, Massachusetts, and Taos and Albuquerque, New Mexico.

And finally, I need to acknowledge my creative influences: Without Sanford Biggers, I would not have linked cultural heritage, visual art and performance, digital media, and mathematics. Hearing Sanford lecture about "historical quilts," "star charts," and "sacred geometry" guided my research. Grandmaster Flash invented scientific techniques that became the backbone of hip-hop culture. Onyx Ashanti's work led me to embodied cognition and creativity, and improvisation, as well as research that links these areas to culturally relevant making.

Preface

Years ago, I taught a course at the College for Public and Community Service (University of Massachusetts, Boston) on multimedia authoring—the ability to combine text, graphics, sounds, and moving images in meaningful ways. One of the required texts was *The Non-designer's Design Book*, specifically the introductory chapter about the author's "Joshua tree epiphany" (R. Williams 2014, 11). In summary, the author learned about the Joshua tree, which was new to her until she went outside and realized that most of the trees on the block were Joshua trees. Once she was aware of the tree— once she could *name* it—she saw it everywhere. The same happened to me when I first encountered STEAM.

That first time was by chance. As a first-year PhD student at Georgia Tech, I was looking for connections to what I was learning in digital media. I found a link between graffiti and mathematics and followed this lead to Ron Eglash at Rensselaer Polytechnic Institute. Ron's work revealed the mathematics in many things I cared about, such as art and hip-hop culture. He wrote about the geometry principles in John Biggers's murals (Eglash 2004), of which I was a fan. Soon after I contacted Ron, I went to an artist talk at Emory University and listened as Sanford Biggers (distant cousin of John) talked

Figure 0.1
The artist Sanford Biggers working in his studio in 2012.
Photo: Nettrice Gaskins. Courtesy of the artist.

about the use of geometry and quilts in his work (figure 0.1). Sanford was very interested in having a conversation (with Ron and
others), and later on I got some support from the National Science
Foundation to make it happen.

Math had become my Joshua tree. At one time in my life, I hated
math because I didn't see how it connected to what I wanted to
do in life, and that was to be an artist. I was unaware of how certain principles in geometry could be found in diverse artworks. I
had felt the same way about computer programming (coding) even
though my mother was a programmer and, at the time, the only
Black woman I knew who did that for a living. I saw how mathematics and computation had inspired John and Sanford Biggers,
as well as some graffiti artists I knew. As my interest in these subjects increased, I hypothesized that something similar might work

to spark the minds of disengaged students in K–12 public schools. Eventually, with the support of Ron Eglash and others, I had a chance to test the theory out.

While all this was happening at Georgia Tech, I enrolled in a non-credit course called the Co-Lab. It was advertised as an experiment, very student driven, very hands on, with no readings or theory. It was a technical-lab meeting to talk about making in a hands-on way. The goals were to briefly introduce certain technologies and to provide examples that highlighted their more advanced use. The technologies in question were Arduino microcontrollers (small, single-input computers), Android devices, and openFrameworks, which is an open-source tool kit designed for creative coding. Suddenly, a new world had opened up to me, but I felt really lonely because I wasn't interested in any projects my fellow students were making.

Other influences showed up around the same time to pique my interest, such as hearing about a young Sierra Leonean inventor named Kelvin Doe, also known as DJ Focus. He reminded me of Grandmaster Flash, a pioneer in the hip-hop culture I felt I was a part of. I met one of my heroes, Hank Shocklee, another hip-hop pioneer who is best known for working with the rap group Public Enemy (I'm still a fan) and the rapper-turned-actor Ice Cube. Hank was in a conference hackerspace making sounds with toys: "circuit bending" involves the customization of circuits within electronic devices such as low-voltage, battery-powered children's toys and digital synthesizers to create instruments (figure 0.2). What Hank was doing reminded me of his innovative use of sampling on rap albums (Bartlett 1994). Then I learned about Onyx Ashanti, who is doing what Hank did but uses his body as the sound-generating instrument (figure 0.3). Their examples led me to further explore maker culture, its performance aspects, and how this relates to creativity and innovation.

Those discoveries and chance meetings that took place when I was doctoral student helped me devise theoretical and conceptual frameworks for techno-vernacular creativity, which also involved

Figure 0.2
The music producer Hank Shocklee with Beatrix Jar in the NAMAC Conference Hackerspace, 2012.
Photo: Nettrice Gaskins.

Figure 0.3
The performer Onyx Ashanti.
Photo: Onyx Ashanti. Courtesy of the artist.

STEAM learning. I did research with students from underrepresented groups across the country. I ran STEAM workshops in Atlanta and taught teachers and students in Boston. Sanford agreed to be a part of the work in Atlanta, and I invited Hank to be a visiting artist at Boston Arts Academy. As a student, I was just trying to merge whom I was becoming and what I loved to do with what I was learning. I wrote this book for students who are as I was: wanting to reach beyond what was being taught in classrooms and be true to themselves and their communities (of practice) in the process.

Introduction

Members of the Freestyle Rap Club gathered every Wednesday in the STEAM Lab at Boston Arts Academy, an urban high school for the visual and performing arts. One week, the legendary hip-hop and electronic music producer Hank Shocklee visited the lab with Matt Johnson of Bare Conductive, a company whose products integrate electronics directly into physical environments. The students in the Freestyle Rap Club designed and built an interactive display of electronic graffiti that, when touched, triggered wall projections of student artwork.

Freestyle rap often includes group protocols. For example, in a call-and-response form of participation, one performer offers a verse and the next performer answers. Participants build on each other's offering and work together to move the performance along and create output that's inventive and collective. When DJ Shocklee and Bare Conductive visited Boston Arts Academy, Shocklee and a student DJ named Moses provided the music, and Daniel, a student emcee, invited members to step into the cypher—an informal gathering of performers—and respond to the beat and to each other, demonstrating their talents and knowledge. The audience touched the conductive paint in the graffiti, triggering sensors on a Touch Board. Each student's turn in the circle was brief—two to three minutes—but packed with action and meaning. In this interactive encounter, the students and club members saw connections among their interest (i.e., hip-hop culture), maker culture, and STEAM learning.

The cypher is an important element of hip-hop culture, providing a structure for sharing knowledge and information readily understood only by those actively engaged in it. The cypher is a place for people to demonstrate and practice their skills, as well as a place to enact self-definition and theorize one's existence in the presence of community. Cyphers represent *kinship-building* practices that are derived from personal or group conceptions of identity, community, and (usually) anticorporate cultures. Kinship suggests the sharing of characteristics or origins, with a shared learning process of working together as a group to achieve common objectives. Dancers, rappers, and other creative *communities of practice* (Lave and Wenger 1991) use the cypher to set group protocols and interactions that include symbols, heroes, rituals, and values from different cultural traditions.

Practitioners from underrepresented ethnic groups have an ontology, or explicit way of being, expressing, creating, or doing things. Using this ontology in STEAM education acknowledges the value of students' experiences and communities, leveraging these as learning platforms for both content and strategy. The cypher is a starting point for a novel STEAM learning approach that encourages students' cultural identity development and supports social justice learning and action. Hosting a rap cypher in the STEAM Lab embeds creative practices in critical pedagogies in ways that challenge mainstream approaches and methods in STEAM education. This book theorizes that activities like the STEAM Lab cypher should be accessible for all students and, moreover, that this type of activity can further engage those who otherwise would not voluntarily participate in making.

As a STEAM Lab activity, the freestyle rap cypher is a *problem space* that encourages creativity, innovation, and real-world problem-solving, such as what happens in established technology centers, makerspaces, and fab labs (digital fabrication laboratories). At Boston Arts Academy, students interacted with each other when performing rap music and with digital artifacts, such as programmable circuit boards that use electronic sensors to trigger animations and sounds (figure 0.4). STEAM Lab staff collaborated with Bare Conductive, the company that makes Touch Boards and Electric Paint, to remix code that enabled students to use the devices in the lab

Figure 0.4
Ninth-grade engineering students presenting Touch Board instruments to Hank Shocklee in the STEAM Lab at Boston Arts Academy, 2015.
Photo: Nettrice Gaskins. Courtesy of Boston Arts Academy.

and outside the lab in engineering classes and in dance and theatrical productions.

Making room for students' cultural practices in standard education points to important dilemmas for educators: How do they balance their students' freedom and creative expression with academic constraints such as testing? Researchers (Archer et al. 2015) are studying the ways that students bring their knowledge, aptitude, skills, and experiences, or capital, into learning settings. For students from groups underrepresented in STEAM, the gap between knowledge and skills is wider than with other groups (Allina 2018). This is a problem that educators are working to solve through culturally relevant teaching and with tools and methods that connect students to where they come from in order to develop more effective ways to support their engagement in STEAM.

Many students from underrepresented groups—African American, Latino/a, and Indigenous—have lived experiences that include uses of STEAM concepts and applications that are different from the formal methods they were taught at school. Sherry Turkle and Seymour Papert (1992) examined the nature of such *epistemological pluralism* in computer science education. Their work looked at the value of different ways of knowing brought by people outside the dominant culture of computer science. The maker movement—a technology-based extension of DIY culture—is still predominantly white and male. Turkle and Papert's research calls into question, not simply dominant practices, but also dominant models that discourage differentiated styles of STEAM teaching and learning. What is considered to be making in dominant culture may be known elsewhere as lowriding, playing and producing music, weaving, or quilting. These latter forms of creativity and innovation represent ways of making and ways of knowing that are often overlooked.

Turkle and Papert's early work challenges dominant STEAM and maker narratives and examines computation in more diverse contexts that include "ordinary" people in their communities making things in different ways from how they were taught in school. This research has implications for STEAM education. For example, computation could enable "concrete" (i.e., culturally relevant) approaches to making in STEAM that conflict with established ways of doing things. Computation—making calculations using step-by-step instructions, or algorithms—when viewed through the lens of culture becomes an expressive tool or medium for the development of diverse perspectives and approaches in dealing with formal and informal STEAM learning and maker spaces.

For over a decade, maker education has gained momentum in schools and out-of-school programs across the United States and the world. For educators, the STEAM and maker movements overlap with the natural inclinations of young people and the power of inventing. Making has the potential to bring greater educational equity for students in public schools and to be a driver in educational and societal change. Often missing from these discussions is how maker practices affect underrepresented ethnic communities. Also absent is recognition of the existing modes and spaces already in these communities, especially ones providing equity of access, inclusion, and relevance for students.

To address these issues, this book expands the definition of making and maker education, connecting technical literacy, equity, and culture through the frame of *techno-vernacular creativity* (TVC), a term that refers to innovations produced by ethnic groups that are often overlooked. This book suggests ways to encourage diversity through epistemological pluralism by identifying and connecting key concepts and tasks. TVC counters the argument that STEAM knowledge is "autonomous and objective, severely downplaying cultural aspects of knowledge production in these fields" (Vakil and Ayers 2019, 450). TVC addresses the tensions and opportunities at play as culturally relevant making is integrated into STEAM instruction.

TVC Modes of Activity

TVC amplifies the creative and cultural practices of underrepresented ethnic groups by addressing the historical and persistent omission in Western schooling contexts of the scientific histories, theories, contributions, and ways of being and knowing that belong to these groups. TVC poses an alternative learning framework and approach that expands the possibility of making by contributing to generative and liberatory experiences for students in different learning settings. TVC builds on the innovations of people who are often overlooked in academic or scholarly discourse, which include African American or Black, Latino/a, and Indigenous communities of practice. TVC demonstrates activities that are context bound, tied to the everyday experiences of practitioners, and constructed using the practitioner's tacit social knowledge, which is rooted in contemporary, culturally relevant making practices.

TVC uses three main modes of activity: reappropriation, remixing, and improvisation. *Reappropriation* is the cultural process by which marginalized or underrepresented ethnic groups reclaim artifacts from dominant culture and the environment. For instance, the Chilean-born, Los Angeles–based artist Guillermo Bert alters and embeds commercial content such as bar codes in textiles made by a community of Indigenous weavers. *Remixing* involves tinkering or making do with whatever is on hand. Early hip-hop DJs used sound-system equipment such as an audio mixer, turntable or record player, and drum machine in ways not intended by the manufacturers.

Improvisation refers to the spontaneous and inventive use of materials and content. Since the arrival of enslaved African people in the Americas, musicians have been using specific techniques to place rhythmic accents between established beats or notes. Juba dancing, also known as the hambone, involves stomping, slapping, and patting different parts of the body. Not limited to music and dance, however, improvisational techniques such as repetition can be applied to visual arts and crafts, such as quilting, that make use of patterns that are amenable to algorithmic modeling. Today's artists and performers use DIY methods to make devices with sensing technology that can be worn on the body or embedded into clothing.

By looking at a broader array of cultural practices, TVC modes can address inequalities in STEAM and making. The persistence of racial/ethnic inequality in the United States is apparent in the *maker movement* (see Vossoughi, Hooper, and Escudé 2016; Quattrocchi 2013). This inequality can work against the natural inclinations of students and the power of *learning by doing* (Martinez and Stager 2019). This book elaborates on TVC as a bottom-up model of STEAM learning, building from implicit skills—for example, collaboration, design thinking, and problem-solving—to explicit knowledge. This approach differs from conventional top-down approaches in which learners acquire explicit knowledge in one subject area and, through practice, turn this knowledge into procedural forms, leading to academic skill-based performances.

A Twenty-First-Century Dilemma in STEAM Education

TVC changes and expands how researchers, scholars, and practitioners conceptualize STEAM, as distinct from claiming that it exemplifies existing or normative ways of thinking about established approaches and skills. TVC prominently positions practitioners in diverse modes of production, especially through remixing, repurposing, and improvising, as well as through computation and digital fabrication. These modes counter dominant ideas about STEAM and who makes in maker culture, as well as how, why, or what they make. To address these ideas, this book expands the definitions of STEAM, making, and maker education—connecting twenty-first-century skills, equity, and culture through the frame of TVC. These practices are not in opposition to formal learning; students from underrepresented groups learn this way when they belong to cultural practices and art forms.

Although a number of scholars and educators within the maker movement have argued the need for more culturally relevant approaches to making, few have developed this work with young people at a higher level of technical depth and creativity. Often missing from these discussions is how maker practices affect African American, Latino/a, and Indigenous groups, as well as girls in and outside of school. The activities of the Boston Arts Academy Freestyle Rap Club demonstrate one example of the potential of culturally relevant making in STEAM and show where, when, and how its members are rooted in diverse epistemologies, therefore contributing to, expanding, and sometimes challenging normative STEAM practices and ways of knowing.

TVC activities can improve school and classroom culture, student-teacher relationships, student engagement, and academic outcomes. Culturally relevant making and STEAM learning tools recognize diverse modes and spaces of making—creating artifacts or tinkering with existing ones—that are familiar to students. TVC connects cultural practices and inventions to STEAM learning through participation and knowledge creation, which contrasts with traditional views of teacher-centered learning through knowledge acquisition.

Culturally relevant educational models emerge from fluid and constantly evolving hip-hop practices (Cooke et al. 2015; Dolberry 2015; Emdin 2010; Love 2012), such as the cypher, that often exist outside the conventional methodological boundaries in formal education. TVC recognizes and describes the creativity and inventiveness of self-taught engineers whose technological innovations were adaptable and flexible enough to influence future developments. It explores customization and Indigenous making that affords transformative and humanizing learning opportunities, which in turn can inform a culturally relevant making practice.

The Power of TVC Making

TVC highlights creative communities of practice and pushes beyond the edges of dominant or mainstream culture. Creators use speculative design (see Dunne and Raby 2014) to produce models and prototypes that serve as "speculation about possible futures . . . and as a catalyst for change." Artists, designers, and inventors create systems and build artifacts that generate new kinds of meanings and perspectives that give a voice to underrepresented ethnic groups.

Issues such as state-sanctioned violence and racial profiling can inspire inventions by young people that counter these actions. Prototyping using digital fabrication (electronics, 3D printing, laser etching) can help students materialize their ideas and counter historically oppressive realities. For example, the Learn 2 Teach, Teach 2 Learn program at the South End Technology Center in Boston, Massachusetts, demonstrated for college students how young people can identify, organize, and integrate information by using hip-hop and social justice as a reference for making things. Teen participants in the program repurposed Adafruit's PianoGlove, which senses colors and visually and aurally re-creates them, to make a color-sensing device that helped wearers appreciate the value of diversity.

The design cypher brings together students, community members, artists, and others to envision translating a cultural practice into technology. To create their devices, the L2TT2L teens learned about electronics, beginning with a design session modeled on the hip-hop cypher, to understand how components such as sensors work. Sensors convert color, heat, light, sound, and motion into electrical signals that are passed through interfaces that convert them into code and passes this on to computers. The input and output process of the sensor was enhanced by the call-and-response feedback loop of the cypher. The teens explored prototyping using rapid cycles of feedback, testing, and evaluation or reflection facilitated their engagement in technology and animated and amplified their ideas of social justice.

Prototyping is a common practice in maker culture. The South End Technology Center example demonstrates how TVC in STEAM provides access points for guiding student inquiry, dialogue, and critical thinking and how it changes or expands DIY making and maker education—connecting technical literacy, diversity, creative expression, and culture.

What's in the Book

The examples provided in this book center TVC practices and inventions that engage underrepresented ethnic students' twenty-first-century ways of knowing and address skills such as creative thinking, problem-solving, and collaboration. Students can develop their capacity to explain and express their ideas to different audiences using their inventions. The book focuses on the rich cultural, contextual, historical, and developmental diversity of STEAM integration and on how making or invention can improve learning and create dynamic learning environments where underrepresented ethnic students feel they belong. A few artists, projects, and artifacts appear more than once to demonstrate important concepts and approaches.

The main part of this book—comprising six chapters about TVC modes—is arranged in three parts that highlight reappropriation, remixing, and improvisation. Each part includes an overview of one of the three practices and includes a chapter that guides research into that practice, followed by one that explores how the practice informs STEAM teaching and learning.

Chapters 1 and 2 are about reappropriation, which engages underrepresented ethnic communities of practice who infuse dominant making with local stylistic elements and reassemble found materials in new ways. As a practice, TVC reappropriation highlights works that can serve as models of competence for educators.

Chapters 3 and 4 cover remixing, which refers to rearranging materials to produce something new. TVC remixing allows learners who have larger repertoires of computational skills to inform strategies to connect cultural practices to STEAM subjects.

Chapters 5 and 6 address improvisation as performance-based creativity and innovation. This includes research in embodied creativity and how this translates into culturally relevant STEAM learning and making.

Chapter 7 explores an equity-oriented approach to making that pays explicit attention to pedagogical philosophies and practices and the ongoing inquiry into the sociopolitical values and purposes of making. The conclusion describes TVC habits of mind and corresponding projects and methods of instruction.

Ground Rules for Key Terms Used in the Book

Certain key terms, which are described below, recur throughout many of the chapters in this book. For example, "remixing" means combining and rearranging existing materials to produce new creative works. Another mainstream use of the term refers to block-based coding software. In this book "remixing" calls on these meanings but also refers to a conceptual framework that forms people's responses to content.

Culture versus Heritage

The term "culture" refers to ideas, customs, and social behaviors of a particular group. "Heritage" refers to aspects of culture that are passed along from one generation to the next, to be preserved for the future. There are examples in the book that refer to the merging of cultures to develop a new culture such as in hip-hop or Afrofuturism. In time, a new culture may become an inherited legacy.

Culturally Relevant versus Culturally Situated

The term "culturally relevant" refers to pedagogy that includes modification of curricula, culture identity development, and social justice learning and action. This book also makes use of the term "culturally situated," which employs computer-based tools to situate designs in specific cultures or cultural practices such as African American quilt making in Gee's Bend, Alabama.

Expert versus Practitioner

In this book, practitioners are experts who use their cultural or Indigenous knowledge as part of their work. This is different from expertise, which can encompass a broad range of characteristics, skills, and ways of knowing. An artist who works with educators in classroom settings might be seen as both a practitioner and an expert.

Indigenous

"Indigenous" refers to ethnic groups who began in a specific place, in contrast to others who have occupied the area more recently. It also refers to individuals or groups who have or share knowledge that is embedded in cultural traditions of local or Indigenous (e.g., Native American, First Nations, Aboriginal) communities.

Underrepresented

In this book, "underrepresented" refers to groups who make up a substantial part of the United States but are less represented in STEAM fields. Some research has been done to address gender gaps in STEAM and making, but fewer studies center the practices and products from African American, Latino/a, and Indigenous communities.

I Reappropriation

1

Self-Taught Engineering, Upcycling, and Speculative Design

Reappropriation encourages the use of imaginative and innovative methods, which is evident in the creation of objects from scrap materials. Self-taught practitioners find a common ground among heritage, aesthetics, and the tradition of using limited resources to channel creativity into value generation. This work is framed by pedagogical theories in culturally relevant making explored by Shirin Vossoughi, Paula Hooper, and Meg Escudé (2016), Vanessa Sheared and Peggy Sissel (2001), and Bill Babbitt, Dan Lyles, and Ron Eglash (2012), along with studies in social innovation (Wegener and Aakjær 2016), DJ methods and sound engineering (Henriques 2011; Fouché 2006), and motorbike and lowrider production (M. Anderson 2017; Chappell 2014; Kanellos 1994), as well as emerging technologies.

TVC reappropriation is defined as the counterhegemonic practice of repurposing things in ways that revalue, resignify, and relocalize artifacts from mainstream, or dominant, cultures. Reappropriation can overlap with remixing because both modes involve the manipulation and use of preexisting artifacts. However, reappropriation is constituted by political transformation as much as it is about object modification. This chapter examines the ways that creative practitioners invent things through TVC reappropriation, especially by infusing dominant maker conventions with Indigenous or local stylistic elements and by reassembling found materials in new ways. The chapter looks at the ways that TVC reappropriation promotes creativity, innovation, and inquiry into the sociopolitical values and purposes of making.

Reappropriation navigates cultural repertoires that are strongly influenced by asymmetrical relationships of power. It demonstrates adaptable ways of making use of existing objects and everyday materials for simple assembly. African American, Latino/a, and Indigenous groups routinely assimilate elements of dominant culture by accepting its forms while drastically altering its content or function—altering European styles of quilting, modifying automobiles, or reproducing sounds using customized sound equipment. Jazz, funk, and rhythm and blues music were all the result of a well-established pattern of reappropriation. For the purposes of this chapter, reappropriation involves the recontextualization of materials and their redeployment, often requiring the reinterpretation of existing technologies while maintaining their traditional uses and forms.

The practice of making do with whatever is on hand is prevalent in disenfranchised or under-resourced communities. TVC reappropriation takes its inspiration from commentary by the Haitian American writer Edwidge Danticat on making through the domestic arts: "If you can't afford clothes, but you can make them—make them. You have to work with what you have, especially if you don't have a lot of money. You use creativity, and you use imagination" (Fassler 2013). Danticat and others make a case for building on the unique contexts of local communities, which extends to culturally relevant making and STEAM learning. These contexts, which are produced in opposition to racialized and gendered hierarchies, often exist outside what is considered to be maker culture.

TVC reappropriation fosters resourcefulness and problem-solving in ways that sustain underrepresented or under-resourced groups. The participatory nature of many of the works described in this chapter give its practitioners a voice that enables them to not feel marginalized (by dominant culture); to make transitions cognitively, developmentally, personally, and socially; to feel a sense of empowerment; to decrease or eliminate stereotypes about who can make things; and to seek new connections and commonalities with others (Sheared 1996). Important issues about race and ethnicity, gender, class, and language are embedded in the act of reappropriating from dominant culture. These issues often intersect and create opportunities for certain groups to embrace their marginalization while "gaining space and voice among those who previously controlled their political, economic, historical and social realities" (Sheared and Sissel 2001, 334).

TVC reappropriation responds to modern globalization while expanding the discourse around innovation, embracing technological methods that disrupt dominant culture as much as they resignify and relocalize objects of mass production. Works highlighted in this chapter provide creative guideposts fueled by the increasing ubiquity of computing and information technology, offering researchers and scholars more opportunities to better understand how practitioners from underrepresented groups reabsorb dominant or mainstream artifacts through a process of creating their own conditions of production as a crucial foundation for reconceptualizing social justice and sustainability (Babbitt, Lyles, and Eglash 2012).

As scholars have noted, some of the most inventive applications of technology come from historically marginalized or under-resourced groups (Mejia and Pulido 2018; Fouché 2006). Practitioners, who are often self-taught, repurpose discarded objects, often inventing new uses for them to meet personal and community needs. "Upcycling" and DIY making are newer contributions to this age-old, global practice. TVC reappropriation chronicles making and the DIY aesthetic among individuals and groups that function at the margins of dominant maker culture but whose works are valued by their communities.

Social Innovation, Social Design Methods, and Tools

Reappropriation fosters innovation, which helps deploy effective solutions to systemic social and environmental issues. The DJ Grandmaster Flash's customization of the audio crossfader, as a *product innovation*, provided a way to control more than one audio source, and his torque theory, as a *process innovation*, allows DJs to find the break of recorded songs by marking vinyl albums with tape or a crayon (Fouché 2006; Vineyard 2014). His quick-mix theory involved finding the break on one turntable, then using an audio mixer to quickly switch to a break on the other. He could also use the mixer to loop one part of a song repeatedly. These and other inventions led to the development of turntablism, which is a *social innovation* that captures how practitioners systematically make use of old ideas as the raw material for new ideas across knowledge domains (Wegener and Aakjær 2016).

TVC reappropriation, as a social innovation, draws attention to inventions that are historically embedded in cultures in which individuals, often by necessity, integrate multiple social identities and practices. This production counters marginalization that occurs when a dominant group's ways of knowing, doing, and learning are valued and voiced at the sociopolitical expense of others (Baatjes 2003). Understanding the multifaceted reality of making can give value and voice to historically marginalized communities of practice that include groups underrepresented in STEAM fields. Members' ability to reappropriate things can, in turn, predict how well and the extent to which they can come up with innovative ideas.

Social innovation—finding solutions to pressing social issues—is in line with situated practices, in which innovative activities are embedded in everyday work and learning. Scholars of local knowledge communities suggest a "unified view" of working, learning, and innovation that looks beyond canonical ideas of practice to capture the rich, multilayered activities of diverse communities

(Brown and Duguid 1991, 40). This includes individuals and groups that do not refer to themselves as makers but do engage in a range of DIY activities related to making that are, according to scholars, rooted in local, cultural, and current making practices, which are situated within opportunities and spaces of transformation (Vossoughi, Hooper, and Escudé 2016).

Taking a unified approach to making requires an exploration of how TVC practitioners add a cultural dimension to social design, providing a mix between upgrading (adding value) and recycling (reuse) in upcycling and the DIY aesthetic that includes innovations that promote a sense of community among practitioners and participants. Researchers (Mejia and Pulido 2018; Emdin 2010, 2007) contend that innovations whose cultural frames of reference may be oppositional to dominant ones may have greater difficulty crossing cultural boundaries. One solution is to advance ways to provide opportunities for participation and inclusion for underrepresented groups and expand the taxonomy of making to value the skills that are gained through TVC reappropriation.

Technologies of Survival in Creative Communities

TVC reappropriation acknowledges underrepresented ethnic groups' ability to adapt new technologies, modifying artifacts on the basis of their political and social circumstances. In Chicano culture, *rasquachismo* signifies the "view of the underdog," which combines inventiveness with a survivalist attitude (M. Anderson 2017). Rasquache practitioners make the most from the least, using discarded and recycled materials, even fragments, to create an aesthetic that is both defiant and inventive. Chicano American lowrider culture demonstrates rasquachismo as a practical application of TVC reappropriation. The technical methods, skills, processes, techniques, tools, and raw materials used in lowrider culture establish an individual or group identity, develop an aesthetic, and fulfill community needs (Chappell 2014).

Lowrider innovation puts a spin on dominant maker practices by reengineering cars with hydraulic automobile suspension systems (figure 1.1). Lowriders play a dynamic role in culturally relevant making, associating the barrio (neighborhood) and its specific ethno-racial identity with engineering (Chappell 2014; Kanellos 1994). Very little research has examined the ways that rasquache forms of expression can be used to teach engineering design. Even less research has been conducted on how the assets of lowriders contribute to the diversification of engineering epistemologies (Mejia and Pulido 2018). Addressing this divide may provide better opportunities for participation and inclusion for Latino/a students and expand taxonomy in engineering education research.

Figure 1.1
A performance of *Symphony 505* in Albuquerque, New Mexico, with Christopher Marianetti, Mary Margaret Moore, and the Down Low Car Club.
Photo: Nettrice Gaskins. Courtesy of ISEA2012.

Acknowledgment of social innovation among urban survivalists extends to African American motorbike culture, which merged mechanical technology and aesthetics. World War II veterans returned home with mechanical skills that they applied to building, modifying, and tinkering with motorcycles (Levingston 2003). For example, Ben Hardy and Cliff Vaughs created iconic customized motorbikes from discarded bikes and found parts (d'Orléans 2014; Wasef 2007). The maker sensibilities of these innovations continue in urban fabrication such as with the DJ Mikal Hameed's "Eames Hotrod Boombox," which merges motorbike and lowrider aesthetics with hip-hop aesthetics and repurposes an Eames lounge chair with electronic components.

Hip-hop creativity and innovation give voice and value to people who make things with fewer resources. Jamaican sound systems—musical amplification and diffusion using electronic components—influenced hip-hop pioneers with West Indian roots, such as the DJ Grandmaster Flash, who were fascinated with tinkering, tearing apart, and reengineering electronic devices to see how they worked (Henriques 2011; Veal 2007). DJ Flash sourced parts from junkyards and repurposed an on-off toggle switch from an old microphone that he then transformed into a device that allowed him to switch from one turntable to another (Fouché 2006).

Urban fabrication through TVC reappropriation reveals a glaring lack of representation in mainstream making circles. The self-taught engineers, tinkerers, and designers from underrepresented groups remain largely unknown and uncredited in mainstream maker outlets such as *Make: Magazine*. Images of making often exclude the aesthetic, vernacular, and spirit of inventiveness that come from the practice of reappropriation. However, it is this work that holds much promise as far as engaging groups that otherwise might not get involved in maker culture. According to Leah Buechley (2014), what contributes to the lack of representation in the maker movement also plagues STEAM fields, in general.

From an insider's perspective, the production of identity in low-rider communities and other creative groups is far more complex and nuanced than appears on the surface. The "bawdy, spunky" sensibility of rasquachismo initiates strategies to "subvert and turn ruling paradigms upside down," re-creating American icons, such as lowrider cars, with "oppositional meaning and function" (Ybarra-Frausto 2011, 294). Practitioners from these groups take ownership in problem-solving, designing, and playing with mechanical and electrical artifacts and in making things. This work can be further emphasized in engineering education to engage students who come with authentic experiences and cultural knowledge.

Culturally Relevant Physical Computing and Prototyping

TVC reappropriation includes *physical computing*, starting with how people express themselves creatively using electronic interfaces and devices. Physical computing can be used to develop constructionist computer science instruction, enabling learners to gain hands-on, or haptic, experiences (Przybylla and Romeike 2014). These experiences include combining wireless communication, devices that measure the acceleration of the body, and musical instrumentation. A growing number of practitioners explore physical computing in equitable ways that acknowledge the importance of diverse cultural representations and identities in embedded systems. Their works demonstrate the development of scientific and computational identities for future STEM growth (Tissenbaum, Sheldon, and Abelson 2019).

Existing tools, platforms, and systems such as contributions by Free Art and Technology (F.A.T.) Lab, Graffiti Research Lab, and openFrameworks are developed by makers who are mostly white males, which makes projects such as Onyx Ashanti's BeatJazz sound system outliers of the mainstream maker movement. Members of F.A.T., Graffiti Research Lab, and openFrameworks formed a team to work with Tony Quan, a graffiti artist also known as Tempt1, who in 2003 was stricken with amyotrophic lateral sclerosis (ALS) and eventually lost all ability to move except using his eyes. The team came up with a solution called EyeWriter.

The EyeWriter team developed an open-source technology solution that allows Tempt1 to communicate to the world using the motion of his eyes. EyeWriter also became a platform for the delivery of Tempt1's unique style of art, which fuses the Los Angeles indigenous cholo writing culture with New York City wildstyle graffiti. *Cholo* means "lowlife," and it was reappropriated by Chicano youth as a popular expression of Mexican American culture. Wildstyle describes a complicated graffiti style constructed with interlocking letters. The EyeWriter device was enhanced by rasquache sensibility through graffiti that is situated in Chicano and hip-hop cultures.

Physical computing can also be used to tell stories. Amelia Winger-Bearskin (2018) embedded meaningful values into Iroquois wampum belts that have symbols and information woven into them to create designs that are authentic to Indigenous practices. Vanessa Ramos-Velasquez's *Coded Narratives* generates stories live via text input from an audience using a tablet PC as a narrative tool and conduit for reappropriation that reuses hardware and software in an experimental way. Wampum conceptualized as decentralized storytelling and software and the *Coded Narratives* performance demonstrate skill in Indigenous craft making, merging hand building and cultural narratives with technology.

Vernelle Noel's work builds on prior work on computational making (see Knight and Stiny 2015) by investigating craft making from Trinidad. Noel explores technology in practices such as wire bending that is the foundation of carnival costume making. Wire benders interpret designs and bend wires into shapes to create frames based on the designs, and these frames are used as supports in costume construction. Noel developed the Bailey-Derek Wire Bending Grammar, which seeks to make the tacit knowledge in wire bending explicit, reuse wire-bending craft in computation, and sustain the art form for future generations (Noel 2015).

Interpreting wire bending through the use of technology shifts traditional designing and crafting to *shape* and *making grammars* that include the construction artifacts and the sensory aspects of making artifacts (Knight and Stiny 2015). Shape grammars are rule-based systems that compute with shapes (Knight and Stiny 2015; Stiny and Gips 1972), and this has been extended to computing (making) with things, especially through *craft performances* such as braiding, weaving, quilting, and other social aspects of design that are "deeply imbued with unique cultural values and expressive of cultural identities" (Knight 2018, 206). These performances are grounded in *constructionism* (Papert 1993), which asserts that learning is an active process in which people construct new knowledge from their everyday experiences. This process is most effective when they are engaged in constructing personally (and culturally) meaningful products.

TVC practitioners make the sociocultural aspects of craft more explicit through reappropriation. The meaning-making and value-generating aspects of reappropriation become foundational in the creation of equitable practices and work. Proponents of the maker movement should include TVC reappropriation as an important way to recognize and nurture what underrepresented ethnic communities of practice value and as a way to insist on dignity and creative expression as guidelines for equity. In every example mentioned here, the creativity and dignity of people who are less considered in mainstream scholarship become the main drivers of innovation and change in their communities and beyond. Projects that involve TVC reappropriation can serve as models of competence for educators and youth practitioners. Also, the examples highlighted in this chapter can guide researchers who explore innovation in STEAM education.

Speculative Design and the Afro Now, Afro Future

TVC reappropriation, social innovation, and social design provide a unified view of creativity, learning, and innovation through value-generating activities that are equitable across cultures. This includes speculative design and technology that make use of physical computing and craft performance. Speculative design involves objects from everyday life and considers the environment and context in which these objects exist (Auger 2013, 12). TVC practitioners use speculative design strategies to connect objects, rituals, and performances and to create spaces and narratives where social justice issues may be brought to light, discussed, and addressed in different ways.

Speculative designs such as W. E. B. Du Bois's fictional "Megascope" (see Du Bois [1905] 2015), paved the way for Afrofuturism and, more recently, the establishment of the Black Speculative Arts Movement (figure 1.2). Afrofuturism is a practice that integrates African diasporic concepts with STEAM subjects in order to interpret, engage, design, or change space and time as a catalyst for the future (R. Anderson 2016). Practitioners who work in this domain explore reappropriation as a *disruptive innovation* that, according to bell hooks (1995), fundamentally connects oppositional practices of the past with forms of resistance in the present to create spaces of possibility for the future. Jazz maverick Sun Ra, an Afrofuturist pioneer, repurposed the materials and metaphors of Cold War science in his artistic practice, which includes DIY instrumentation, electronic costumes, and multimedia performances. These developments task makers to think critically about the future, the devices they will use, and the relationship between power and cultural production.

Practitioners who channel Afrofuturism explore inquiry-based learning, or the use of prompts, in a design process like that implemented by *Iyapo Repository*, which takes an ecological approach to connect objects, rituals, and performances to create spaces and narratives where social justice issues are brought to light, discussed, and

Figure 1.2
"Megascope" by Stacey Robinson.
Photo: Stacey Robinson. Courtesy of the artist.

addressed. Facilitators and conservators created this archive to collect ideas from participants and turn them into digital prototypes and, occasionally, into physical artifacts that affirm and project the future of the African diaspora. Participants are provided with color-coded cards and prompts. Participants complete a field notes worksheet that, according to facilitators, follows questions such as

> What kind of a future is this artifact for: dystopian, utopian, apocalyptic, or revolutionary? Which cultural arena does the artifact engage: music, politics, fashion, space travel, security, education, or health? . . . A third tag asks for more detailed description: does the object have a motor, transmit data, permit wear, make sound, change color, or serve for self-defense? (Schmid 2017)

TVC reappropriation in Afrofuturism fosters self-sufficiency by coming up with new and different ways to engage with mathematics, science, engineering, and technology. Amiri Baraka imagined a new kind of technology, an "expression-scriber" into which he could "step & sit or sprawl or hang & use not only my fingers to make words express feelings but elbows, feet, head, behind, and all the sounds I wanted, screams, grunts, taps, itches . . . the xpression, three dimensional—able to be touched, or tasted or felt, or entered, or heard or carried like a speaking singing constantly communicating charm" (1971, 157). Decades later, Baraka's vision became Afrofuturist artifacts such as Ayodamola Okunseinde's "Afrofuturist Lantern" (*Iyapo Repository* Artifact #25), an ambient data storytelling device (figure 1.3). BeatJazz was featured in *Make: Magazine* and highlighted by SparkFun Electronics in 2014, which is an increasingly popular website in the maker community.

The artist Stephanie Dinkins uses artificial intelligence (AI) to generate new and repurpose existing content. "Not the Only One" (N'TOO) tells the story of an African American family though voice-driven AI that builds a story about family, sacrifice, survival, and self-preservation. To make this AI robot storyteller, Dinkins recruited coders and creative technologists from underrepresented

Figure 1.3
"Afrofuturist Lantern" by Ayodamola Okunseinde.
Photo: Ayodamola Okunseinde. Courtesy of the artist.

communities who repurposed text from Toni Morrison's *Sula* and family interviews (as data) to test the AI, which was required to train storytelling algorithms (as output). "N'TOO" shows social innovation through networking and problem-solving by building a community of practice around the use of AI and art. Dinkins noted,

> For us, it's an archive, it [answers] where did you come from? . . .
> I love what people [ask it]. The other day someone walked up to it
> and said "Black lives matter." I love that somebody asked it about
> its grandmother. People ask it general questions like "why do you
> exist?" (Dooley 2019)

"N'TOO" and similar projects have the potential for helping people see themselves as "capable of designing and implementing computational solutions to self-identified problems or opportunities" (Tissenbaum, Sheldon, and Abelson 2019, 35). UK-born Shantell Martin, like Stephanie Dinkins, used AI as machine learning, which involves the creation of algorithms that can learn from and make predictions based on data. Martin collaborated with a computer science student to explore pattern recognition in AI. "Mind the Machine" is an attempt to rehumanize the concept of the algorithmic process and to uncover elements of the artist's identity (Gaskins 2017). Martin installed a robotic plotter driven by a Raspberry Pi, a small, single-board computer that issues algorithmically generated drawings that simulate her style of drawing (figure 1.4).

Wearable technology such as Okunseinde's "Afrofuturist Lantern" takes into account clothing and accessories, home furnishings, and other objects that include embedded computational and electronic elements (Buechley 2013). The emergence of this domain engages girls in computer science and engineering by integrating artistic processes as well as a more playcentric approach to technology and

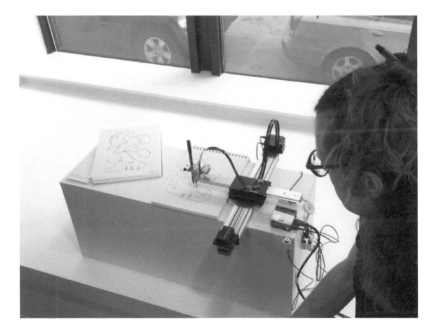

Figure 1.4
"Mind the Machine" robotic plotter that created art using an algorithm based on Shantell Martin's marker drawings.
Photo: Nettrice Gaskins. Courtesy of the artist.

engineering education (Reimann 2011). Cree designer Angel Aubichon created a dress called "The Matriarch Speaks," featuring a traditional Indigenous design with fringe that lights up with the wearer's heartbeat. The garment presents Aubichon's identity through computational action. This development connects to recent work with culturally situated design tools, especially the incorporation of algorithmic design and electronics in heritage artifacts such as quilts (Bennett 2016).

Through TVC reappropriation, practitioners become actively engaged in emerging engineering and computational design processes with an eye to the future in which those who are historically marginalized and under-resourced can innovate and solve problems; adapt and show creative ways of repurposing objects by making use of everyday materials; and speculate about themselves and the world, using heritage and history to repurpose technology and make new things. Their works are characterized as making something out of nothing and are designed on the basis of future imaginaries that are structured by resourcefulness. The next chapter explores educational strategies that draw on TVC reappropriation practices and explore projects that foster curiosity, motivation, and engagement.

2
Hitting Switches and the Hero's Journey

At Dramatic Results, an educational nonprofit in Long Beach, California, twenty teachers from different schools attended a two-hour professional development workshop to learn how to engage students using a culturally relevant STEAM approach. The teachers were introduced to the TVC Maker Toolkit and explored TVC reappropriation by using found materials to make objects of interest and other methods. During the workshop facilitators emphasized the importance of recognizing cultural practices and how these practices can help teachers develop STEAM curricula to increase student motivation. Teachers created their own design maps. For example, one group came up with a wearable defense device based on Medusa from Greek mythology. They added design constraints for the device and cultural references, and they developed brainstorming questions for students.

The Long Beach teachers were invited to observe a three-hour STEAM workshop led by the workshop facilitator at Lindbergh Middle School with twenty-one sixth-grade students who explored Afrofuturism and biomechanics—the study of mechanical concepts relating to the movement of living beings—and fictional cyborgs and real people whose physical abilities are enhanced. Examples included comic book characters such as Marvel Universe's Cyborg. Participants watched videos about real-life cyborgs such as the BeatJazz performer Onyx Ashanti and the Los Angeles graffiti artist Tempt1. These examples were used to strengthen students' exposure to and knowledge of science and technology, as well as recognize the innovations of practitioners from African American, Latino/a, and Indigenous communities.

TVC challenges commonplace assumptions about who is a maker and what constitutes a maker practice, and it addresses ways to effectively teach culturally relevant making through TVC reappropriation that creates an opening for *differentiated instruction* (see Santamaria 2009) that includes a range of different avenues for understanding habits otherwise known as the *maker mind-set* (Martin 2015). This mind-set includes values, beliefs, and dispositions that are common in the mainstream maker community. Cultural practices that involve making but are not labeled as such by the creators provide opportunities for exploring methods that can be implemented to address gaps in student interest and motivation.

The STEAM workshop at Lindbergh Middle School explored the maker mind-set by designing devices for biomechanical cyborgs on the basis of Afrofuturism and TVC reappropriation. This production includes practitioners who adopt technology as part of their identity. For example, Onyx Ashanti recycles found objects and electronic components to prototype sound systems that are worn on the body. Practitioners also design devices that solve problems, such as EyeWriter for the disabled artist Tempt1. The goal at Lindbergh was to demonstrate African American, Indigenous, and Latino/a student interest and engagement in authentic maker practices using methods such as the following.

Design Briefs

Design briefs, as a guided inquiry method, allow teachers to be clearer about their expectations, introduce concepts, and provide information. Lindbergh sixth graders were given a *design brief* that outlined the deliverables and scope of the project, including problems to solve, design constraints, materials, and tasks to accomplish. One of the key tasks was to develop a design (concept) map to visually represent their knowledge and show the relationships between different concepts or ideas. Students learned about levers in biomechanics such as muscle *effort*, the *load* (or weight of the body), and the *fulcrum* (or joint). They took notes while watching videos about cyborgs in popular culture and real life (figure 2.1). In their groups, the students were given flip chart paper and pencils to draw their chosen cyborg models. Students added to their design maps by connecting their models to one or more ideas (figure 2.2). Groups presented their maps and talked about the next phase: creating a prototype.

Figure 2.1
Lindbergh Middle School students take observational notes while discussing ideas.
Photo: Nettrice Gaskins. Courtesy of Lindbergh Middle School.

Figure 2.2
Students in a design mapping activity at Lindbergh Middle School.
Photo: Nettrice Gaskins. Courtesy of Lindbergh Middle School.

Models and Demonstrations

Design mapping provides a scaffold and centers student knowledge as a way to define the why behind making a prototype and addresses how to implement the design brief. Models and demonstrations can set the scene, especially through cultural modeling—scaffolding cultural knowledge to support discipline-specific learning—and showing students what could be done. Lindbergh sixth graders practiced close looking (further explained in chapter 4) with a working prototype of a cyborg hand made of found objects that included cardboard, drinking straws, and rubber bands. Fishing line connected actuators (servos) to the fingers, and an Arduino controlled the hand's movements (figure 2.3). The model prototype presented to the Lindbergh students met the criteria of the design brief and provided students with a place to start tinkering.

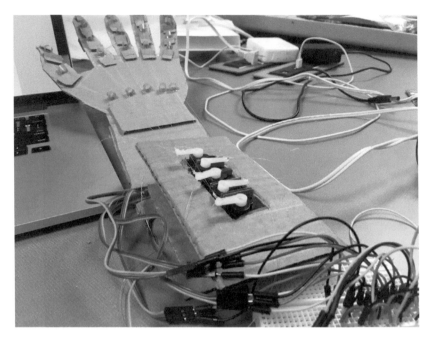

Figure 2.3
Model of a working biomechanical cyborg prototype.
Photo: Nettrice Gaskins. Courtesy of Lindbergh Middle School.

Technological Doodling and Thinkering

Reappropriation overlaps with remixing, which is explored later in
the book, through meaning making and *modular prototyping* to help
students think creatively and problem solve issues. Lindbergh students were actively engaged in making sense of their design briefs—
the models, inventions, relationships—drawing on available materials
and cultural resources (figure 2.4). Modular prototyping acts on discrete things that can be readily repurposed. This method links sepa-
rating and combining components to *technological doodling*, which
explores problem-solving with technology (Dixon 2015; Turkle and
Papert 1992). Students were given time to doodle with the materials,
technologies, and tools made accessible to them. They learned how to

Figure 2.4
Students "thinkering" with found materials to create their biomechanical cyborg prototype at Lindbergh Middle School.
Photo: Nettrice Gaskins. Courtesy of Lindbergh Middle School.

"build to think," which enabled them to break down project tasks into steps based on their level of knowledge (Macdowell 2015, 170). The *thinkering* process can include the use of digital prototyping tools such as Makey Makeys (invention kits), Micro Bits, or Love to Code microcontrollers to add electronic components to their projects.

Collaborative Peer Review

When developing STEAM projects teachers can look at cyborg prototyping and other examples such as *hip-hop architecture*, which uses the *design cypher* to challenge young people to explore hip-hop culture as a way to better understand, conceive, and create architecture (Cooke et al. 2015). Design mapping and *peer reviews* also integrate the hip-hop cypher into the design thinking process to create innovative solutions to prototype. Using a collaborative peer review approach, Lindbergh students presented prototypes that included a mechanical hand inspired by a real-life cyborg artist who sees colors, rocket legs based on cyborg characters in comics, and a remixed EyeWriter for disabled cyborg girls.

The peer review activity at Lindbergh consisted of a twenty-minute *gallery walk*, with each group providing constructive critiques for their cyborg prototypes. Facilitators numbered each group's design maps and left blank worksheets with corresponding numbers next to each prototype. Groups answered worksheet questions about the prototypes, in rounds. They were instructed to move to the closest project, answer the questions for ten minutes, leave the completed worksheet, and move on to the next project when instructed, repeating the process until every prototype was reviewed (figure 2.5). Groups were given enough time to read and discuss their peers' feedback on the worksheets such as the following:

Question 1: What things do you see? Describe the elements in the work.
Group member 1: I see a diagram and a phone, also there are glasses.

Question 2: How are science and technology elements used in the project?
Group member 2: Foil, cardboard, straws, tape, phone, diagram, and tissue paper.

Question 3: How does the project convey the overall theme?
Group member 3: The theme was cyborg, and they used tech.

Question 4: Do you like this project? Why or why not?
Group member 4: Yes. The project was creative.

Crossing the Gulf of Expertise

Traditionally trained educators may struggle with the maker mindset because it requires more flexibility and innovation in their

Figure 2.5
Students engaged in a peer review and gallery walk at Lindbergh Middle School.
Photo: Nettrice Gaskins. Courtesy of Lindbergh Middle School.

application of procedural knowledge. Many traditional educators teach and assess factual knowledge using closed-ended problem-solving techniques specific to a particular discipline, which, according to scholars, is unsuited for teaching design skills for open-ended problems that may involve multiple disciplines (Martin et al. 2015). Being more flexible and adaptable in the approach to STEAM learning can motivate students to interact with new subjects or materials (Mercier and Higgins 2013). Teachers, as adaptive experts, can help students cross the *gulf of expertise* (see Nasir et al. 2005) to move to more complex problems as students gain more knowledge.

Adaptive expertise encourages students to brainstorm and address changes as their projects develop, whether with materials or technical and design limitations, helping students put learning in new or different contexts (Hatano and Oura 2003). Adaptive experts help students develop key competencies in making, allowing them to develop concrete, tangible, and real-world projects that come from their imaginations. TVC reappropriation adds the dimensions of culture and social innovation by highlighting projects that bring attention to works embedded in students' cultures and communities and connect to subjects such as mechanical engineering, which combines physics and mathematics principles with materials science to design and make things.

Teachers at Hayden Community High School in Phoenix, Arizona, started a robotics program to encourage hands-on engineering learning and engage their students in quick, outside-the-box thinking to solve problems. Applying the teachers' adaptive expertise in science (computer science and engineering) helped increase their students' science capital, which included knowledge about Mexican cultural practices, and demonstrated TVC reappropriation in robotics. Featured in the documentary *Underwater Dreams*, the Hayden underwater robotics team entered a competition and defeated every team, including one from MIT (Kim 2015).

After the film was screened at the Museum of Science in Boston, panelist and former Hayden robotics team member Lorenzo Santillana mentioned "hittin' switches," which, in lowrider vernacular, refers to changing the ride height of a vehicle at the flick of a switch (Gab 2016). The winning Hayden team demonstrated flexibility and inventiveness when their robot sprang a leak during the first day's practice run, solving the issue by using tampons to plug their electronics box. It could be argued that having a "bicultural sensibility" (see Ybarra-Frausto 2019) helped the students bridge different methods and be more flexible in problem-solving.

TVC Reappropriation and Invention Education

The Hayden engineering teachers' approach supported their students' exposure to and knowledge about rasquachismo and lowrider culture through *cultural scaffolding* (see Quintana et al. 2004), in which learners can actively engage in authentic practice in productive ways to cross the gulf of expertise. Cultural-scaffolding activities are organized around sensemaking—a process by which people give meaning to their collective experiences—using concepts to bridge learners' understanding and organizing tools and artifacts around themes and STEAM subjects. TVC reappropriation supports a novel approach to engage students in this process, beginning with self-selecting culturally relevant problems to solve. This approach includes collaboration, iterative learning, and invention through connected communities.

Integrating TVC reappropriation into STEAM learning can be instrumental in efforts to balance power. Reappropriation is linked to "reclamation," a term that is used with respect to vernacular. To "reclaim" literally means to make one's own, or to regain, retrieve, recover, repossess, salvage, or rescue (Godrej 2011). Historically, technological innovation has politically, socially, and intellectually silenced certain groups and in the worst cases rendered them defenseless and invisible (Fouché 2006). Students from underrepresented ethnic groups learn that, by reclaiming or reappropriating artifacts, they can refashion the meanings to correspond with particular academic goals. This gives innovative projects the authority of student ownership.

As noted by Amanda Murray, sometimes a culture of innovation "blossoms as a product of its environment, nurtured by the physical and ideological elements of a place . . . and sometimes innovation flourishes in spite of its surroundings" (2010; ellipsis in original). Hip-hop started in the grim backdrop of the Bronx, New York, during the 1970s, and in less than a decade the culture had spread to practitioners around the world. As a practice, hip-hop inspires people to problem solve, take risks, and innovate with sound, audio mixing, and devices that sample, loop, and repeat rhythms or beat patterns. Hip-hop innovation shifted the value of consumer goods that primarily benefited commercial manufacturers to locally made inventions that sustain local communities and the products they value.

Hip-hop as a social innovation predates invention education, a mainstream initiative that has joined educational efforts such as making, coding, robotics, and entrepreneurship in bringing integral elements into the K–16 curriculum. Research shows the link between invention education and students' increased enthusiasm for entrepreneurship, innovation, and engineering; capacity for teamwork; and basic business acumen (Moore et al. 2017). Invention education gives students a personal context and application for STEM and design knowledge. In contrast to invention education, culturally relevant making and culturally situated design resist "value extraction," or the commodification of cultural production (Eglash and Garvey 2014, 77).

TVC reappropriation centers practitioners as value generators who create their own conditions of product and process innovation. Their contributions show the importance of iteration, or repetition, in the invention process. Hip-hop practitioners made a significant contribution to the development of the crossfader, sampler or beat machine, and audio mixer. They use devices to repeatedly loop audio sequences to prolong a beat. The reuse of existing recordings to sample, cut, scratch, and loop sequences are all methods of invention and integral to hip-hop aesthetics and innovation.

Some scholars (see Ryoo et al. 2015) focus on an equity-oriented approach of iterative, continuous improvement that involves making things that require time and resources, including access to materials and knowledgeable experts who are willing to support students during the *creative failure* process. Creative failure requires an understanding among teachers that students may try and fail several times to reach their destinations. Other scholars (Estabrooks and Couch 2016; Smith and Henriksen 2016) suggest that embracing failure is part of the invention process, especially in art classrooms. Invention flourishes in dedicated spaces inside and outside school to help students make the connection from STEAM to the real world. Finding projects that motivate students to accept creative failure is a challenge.

At Boston Arts Academy, the STEAM Lab became a resource for students who needed to find more challenging projects. Referred to the lab by their music teacher, a group of students entered the space with a problem: making a MIDI sound box to compose music with. MIDI (musical instrument digital interface) is a protocol that allows instruments to communicate with other devices. Searching for how to build an open-source MIDI controller, the students found a tutorial on the Adafruit website that was broken into smaller, more manageable parts (Burgess 2014) (figure 2.6). The students required

Figure 2.6
High school music majors create MIDI controllers in the STEAM Lab at Boston Arts Academy as part of their independent study.
Photo: Nettrice Gaskins. Courtesy of Boston Arts Academy.

the assistance of lab staff to problem solve through learning by iteration, or trial and error. For the rest of the semester, students learned about circuit design and soldering, 3D printing, laser cutting, and coding Arduinos.

The invention process that engaged these students used TVC reappropriation to break a project into sequences, parts, or modules to be rearranged or reassembled to create something new that can be reflected upon and shared with others. BAA students learned about Prince's customization of the Linn LM-1 drum machine (C. Johnson 2017). They reported that listening to the song "777-9311" (performed by Prince) motivated them to work through challenges. This example centered students' personal interests and cultural knowledge in ways that connect to learning theories of making with a view that tinkering is informed and iterative, thereby allowing answers to be derived from mistakes (Martinez and Stager 2019). Projects like the MIDI controller start students on a journey. Along the way they find support from adaptive experts, as when teachers help them grapple with challenging tasks such as soldering and coding printed circuit boards, and they learn how iterations of failure can lead to success.

The Hero's Journey and Simple Machines

Students involved in maker and STEAM activities will see the invention process as a journey toward achievement or success. Their teachers may have them explore unfamiliar topics such as biomechanics by using familiar cultural representations—for example, the *hero* in the hero's journey, a literary motif that has been repeated across stories and cultures, becoming a shared experience for many people (Georgas, Regalado, and Burgess 2017). The journey begins with a call to adventure—a challenge that must be undertaken—that disrupts the comfort of the potential hero's ordinary world. For students who are underrepresented in STEAM, the call will begin the moment they step into a designated maker space.

The hero's journey, as a metaphor for culturally relevant maker activities in STEAM learning, tells the story of student heroes who embark on a journey, bringing along their capital—values, attitudes, expectations, and behavior—which influences how they view themselves and the maker process. In the STEAM Lab, the learning process looks like this: First, the student hero—who enters as a novice—receives a call to adventure from a messenger or teacher whose role is to help in the conceptual understanding of a particular task. This interaction can encourage the student hero to come up with ideas for new solutions to problems as well as the procedures for solving them.

There may be a moment of hesitation or denial, which is the refusal of the call; the student hero's anxiety is relatable to many people who are trying something new. At this point, a mentor or adaptive expert emerges to reassure the student hero and offer tools, materials, or advice to aid him or her. This phase is critical because the student hero will need motivation to continue the journey. Each student hero will quickly assess whether the project or assignment is interesting, relevant, or worth learning. Heroes may also want to know whether the project will open the door to other opportunities or help them reach a goal.

The second stage of the journey begins when student heroes cross the threshold into an unknown world in which they need to complete a series of tests, or a long road of trials, often with the help of allies such as teachers, mentors, and peers. During this stage students may experience creative failure. To keep them from getting lost in a strange domain (the unknown), they will have general guidelines to follow. Design briefs prevent students from being drained of creative possibilities or discouraged from continuing. With proper support, student heroes can overcome failure, seeing creativity and innovation as a long-term, cyclical process of small successes and frequent mistakes.

Teachers can invoke the hero's journey with the imperative for students to frame the design process as a personal and meaningful one rather than following a strict set of guidelines or completing tasks the way students think the teacher wants them to. Using the example of the hero's journey, teachers can challenge students to select projects that foster their genuine curiosity and interest. Teachers can encourage students to ask research questions and scan the environment to seek answers. Students can repurpose existing content to come up with new ideas, crossing from the unknown into the known with projects that are of value to them.

The metaphor of the hero's journey is part of *The Boy Who Harnessed the Wind*, a film and memoir (see Kamkwamba and Mealer 2010) about a young Malawian inventor who dabbled in fixing radios for his friends and neighbors and spent his free time looking through the local junkyard for salvageable electronic components. William Kamkwamba found a mentor in his science teacher, who indirectly led him to the school library, where he read about electrical engineering and energy production. Kamkwamba's call to adventure began with a drought and the resulting famine that devastated his village, leading to riots over rationing and Kamkwamba's family being robbed of their already dwindling grain stores.

Once he crossed the threshold, Kamkwamba himself was tested after facing and overcoming obstacles that spurred him into action: he created a windmill prototype and used the scale model to solicit support from allies and friends. This hero story demonstrates not only the inventiveness of a largely self-taught engineer and maker but also the social justice possibilities of making in struggling communities. The story shows the positive loop of innovation and prototype development. In it an informal learning hangout is established where youths gather and share ideas and reinterpret the possibilities of repair and waste: "The snake bites its tail; fractal complexities grow as one-to-one skill-sharing builds up to small working groups . . . and ultimately perhaps a community of maker spaces that share materials, practices and projects" (Eglash and Foster 2014, 13).

Strategies for Culturally Relevant Design Thinking

At the Autodesk Technology Center in Boston, Massachusetts, English-language arts (ELA) teachers from Boston Latin Academy and Madison Park Technical Vocational High School formed a team to address this overarching question: *How might we provide kids with strategies for culturally relevant design thinking across disciplines?* As part of the Autodesk–Boston Public Schools fellowship, the teachers spent three weeks learning how to use Autodesk software such as Tinkercad and equipment such as 3D printers, design a curriculum using the software and equipment, and give a presentation for Autodesk staff and Boston Public Schools administrators and teachers. The ELA teachers experienced their own hero journey at Autodesk, where for the first time they had access to expertise, maker materials, and digital tools for STEAM learning.

At the end of the introductory training, the ELA teachers experienced a moment of hesitation when they wondered how they could create ELA lessons with what they were learning at the Autodesk center. With support from Autodesk and experts from Boston schools, they decided to repurpose Homer's *Odyssey* and the Rube Goldberg machine. The intended outcome of the project was for ninth-grade students to be able to illustrate the hero's journey from the *Odyssey* by designing a machine comprising a series of simple devices that link together to produce a domino effect—each device triggers the next one. The goal of the Rube Goldberg machine is achieved after all the simple machines are triggered (Wolfe 2000).

At the Autodesk center, the teachers had crossed the unknown threshold, where they were challenged to be open about what was possible for their classrooms. Every year public schoolteachers and administrators are pressured to show results with student grades and test scores. Traditional pathways to teaching are often siloed in specific academic subjects, discouraging the integration of other subjects such as art and technology. Designing a curriculum that includes other disciplines was unfamiliar territory to ELA teachers and, facing the unknown, they were being asked to develop a maker mind-set and gain new skills in 3D modeling and digital manufacturing using the Autodesk software and center equipment.

For the teachers, the revelation that changed how they viewed the project came when they saw how simple machines such as planes, levers, wedges, wheels and axles, pulleys, and screws could be used to illustrate ELA concepts by having students write words to link the major sections of the *Odyssey* to descriptions for each simple machine. For example, a student may describe a lever as "a rod that turns on a pivot, or fulcrum," and then connect this description to Zeus weighing Odysseus's fate in his scales. In addition to or in the place of the *Odyssey*, students can explore culturally relevant examples of the hero's journey in *Black Panther*, *Papa John's Tall Tale*, and *Kirikou and the Sorceress*.

After creating design maps for their Rube Goldberg machines, students could begin the maker stage, which includes the use of found materials: paper, newspaper, toilet paper rolls, balls, marbles, blocks, toy cars, ramps, rocks, glue, wire, fabric, books, scissors, tape, markers, and so on. The ELA teachers developed other ideas such as having students redesign the gift-giving experience of the hero's journey for their peer or teammate. Tasks for this design challenge include interviews, sketching ideas based on their peers' needs, building a solution, sharing their prototype, and getting peer feedback.

Broadening the Maker Mind-Set

Maker activities and habits of mind that are inclusive can help students see connections between themselves and the dominant world. TVC reappropriation gives students a stake in choosing among topics provided for them by showing them how cultural practices and their lived experiences are part of the process of making. One example is *technologies of the heart,* an approach that "brings out the best in humanity and enhance[s] personal relationships" (Klimczak 2016, 61). This includes using the humanities to develop maker mind-sets by using Scratch programming, programmable circuit boards, and electronic components.

South End Technology Center's Learn 2 Teach, Teach 2 Learn (L2TT2L) program helps youth reappropriate or, as artist Xenobia Bailey refers to it, "funk" things together by looking at how communities of practice solve problems with limited resources (Graves 2011). L2TT2L youth design projects that are, as described by Amiri Baraka, "three dimensional—able to be touched, or tasted or felt, or entered, or heard or carried" (1971, 157). They become aware of projects such as Ayodamola Okunseinde's "Artifact:025," mentioned previously, which vibrates as a way to alert wearers when they are at the cross street of a police-involved shooting in New York City, a reminder of why Black lives matter.

L2TT2L youth address community issues such as the pressure schoolteachers and students feel to not speak about state-sanctioned violence in their communities. The L2TT2L program came up with the "Making Liberation" project to link the iterative engineering design process with Black Lives Matter activists' deployment of call-and-response participation to organize protests. "Making Liberation" participants were given the time and space to explore inventions like Grandmaster Flash's modification of the crossfader. They learned spontaneity and improvisation through graffiti and spoken word poetry to express their thoughts and feelings about racial pro-filing and police brutality.

"Making Liberation" recruited mentors from the local commu-nity to engage youth in design cyphers (see Cooke at al. 2015), col-laborative peer reviews, and the reappropriation or translation of cultural practices into technologies of the heart. As mentioned in the introduction, one L2TT2L group repurposed Adafruit's Piano-Glove to explore social justice, diversity, and inclusion (figure 2.7). They presented their Rainbow Glove to community members as part of a cypher activity to show how physical computing can con-vey a message. They related a story about using the device to explore

Figure 2.7
Learn 2 Teach, Teach 2 Learn youth teach graduate education students about the Rainbow Glove and the cypher at Harvard University in Cambridge, Massachusetts. Photo: Nettrice Gaskins. Courtesy of the South End Technology Center.

what sounds were generated by different skin colors, emphasizing the importance of diversity to create melodies.

What readers can take away from this chapter is that TVC reappropriation, as a social innovation and practice, creates opportunities for educators to create intentional instruction that challenges assumptions about who is a maker and what constitutes a maker practice. TVC reappropriation gives students agency by acknowledging the value of their cultural knowledge, prior experiences, and creativity through the use of culturally relevant making strategies that connect to STEAM concepts. These strategies help teachers negotiate maker and classroom cultures with their students, reflect the communities where students develop and grow, and address students' sociocultural realities and histories.

II   Remixing

3

Conceptual Remixing and Computation

This chapter addresses remixing—adding, removing, and changing artifacts—which is a key element of TVC, and is foundational to understanding TVC as a critical pedagogy. Remixing as a TVC mode expands on the work of scholars such as Karyn Recollet (2016), Martin Irvine (2014), and Eduardo Navas (2012) and links their work to open-source and online programming tools (Eglash et al. 2006; Bennett 2016; Dasgupta et al. 2016) and culturally relevant making (Elkordy and Keneman 2019; Vossoughi, Hooper, and Escudé 2016). This chapter also looks at the work of educators, scholars, theorists, artists, and practitioners not normally considered in critical pedagogy discourse (Wynter 1992; Rose 1994; Dery 1994; Cheliotis and Yew 2009; Banks 2011). Last, the chapter considers remixing in art and the emergence of computational thinking (see Wing 2016) and computational action (Tissenbaum, Sheldon, and Abelson 2019) to position TVC remixing in emerging educational discussions.

TVC remixing provides a platform from which the practitioners act as *value generators* for their communities. Remixing generates artifacts of value that are largely circulated and enjoyed within communities of practice (Eglash and Garvey 2014). Cultural expressions and artifacts associated with remixing emerge from generative processes for meaning making that underlie many cultural symbolic systems (Irvine 2014). Take, for example, *call-and-response*, which comes from African and Indigenous oral traditions (Smitherman 1977) and sets up creative works in such a way that pieces begin to function as questions and answers to each other. Participants can be part of a cypher where everyone is invited to join in. The facilitator (e.g., emcee, DJ, or VJ) provides content for performers to respond to. Participants familiar with the process or flow can respond and contribute to the overall project. The process is algorithmic because the underlying structure responds to commands, patterns, or instructions.

Remixing, which is not a new or strictly technological practice, includes practices that have been amplified by widespread access to computer technology, whereby existing works are rearranged, combined, or remixed into a new work: a song, section of artwork, block of code, book, video, or lesson plan can all be remixed. The scholar Sylvia Wynter (1992) describes remixing as a *deciphering practice* that highlights systems of meaning and attempts a *transvaluation of values*. As a way to convert information into new forms, remix practitioners alter or subvert dominant themes and represent concepts in an entirely different light on the basis of their unique lived experiences, points of view, and identities.

Working with minimal resources, TVC pioneers—artists, producers, and performers—use remixing to impose their creative will on mainstream society (Watkins 2008, 28). DJs and sound engineers, who are part of a collective of creative practitioners, frequently sample from existing songs, capturing what James A. Snead (1990) describes as the principles of rhythm, repetition, and collage. Practitioners remix through *cutting*, or alternating between duplicate copies of the same record, and *scratching*, which involves moving a vinyl record beneath a turntable needle to create a "real-time, live-action collage" (B. Williams 2002). Practitioners' aesthetic impulse to remix content through repetition includes an iterative process of returning to a previous series or sequence in a song or mix before continuing the performance.

In the following sections we look at how TVC remixing is used in visual art, craft, performance, and computational making.

Remixing in Hip-Hop

In hip-hop, remixing is linked to the discourse of repetition and to the embodied memories of dispossession and resistance (Coleman 2009; Snead 1990). *Turntablism* is an invention that was developed by early hip-hop DJs and immigrant music "selectors" from the Caribbean who brought dub—music without vocals—and dance remixing to the United States, where hip-hop was born. Cutting, scratching, and sampling involves the manipulation of sounds, sound effects, and rhythms or beats by using one or more turntable record players and a crossfader audio mixer. However, few scholars and researchers refer to these techniques as forms of computational thinking or examine computational tools that link remixing to communities of practice whose influences are unnoticed.

Grandmaster Flash, a Bronx-based DJ with Barbados origins, is known for using scientific and engineering processes (see Fouché 2006) that involve turntablism, which illustrates that, for African Americans and other underrepresented ethnic groups, technological innovation has been an important means of creative expression. DJ Flash is known for inventing DJ techniques such as "punch phrasing," which involves isolating, then rhythmically punching in short segments of songs using an audio mixer. Flash's inventions paved the way for DJs who used remixing as a way to combine different concepts, artifacts, and technology to make something new.

Hip-hop became a global phenomenon, reaching parts of the world where self-taught practitioners as value generators, with access to low-cost, free, or open-source tools and technology, could make music and devices that circulate value in their communities. In their chosen creative practices, DJs also use cut and copy-and-paste techniques offered by video editing machines and computer software applications (Navas 2012, 4). DJ Spooky remixed other forms of media such as D. W. Griffith's 1915 film *Birth of a Nation*. Self-taught inventor Kelvin Doe managed his own radio station in Sierra Leone where he played music under the moniker DJ Focus (Landry 2012). Like DJ Flash, Doe (Focus) tinkered with discarded pieces of scrap to build equipment. DJ Flash, DJ Spooky, and DJ Focus—linked by the multifarious connective tissues of TVC production—are not necessarily examples of the same knowledge culture or value system, but all can be seen as challenging dominant cultural paradigms in unique ways.

Remix Scholarship

Scholars have different ideas about what remixing is. Eduardo Navas defines the remix as a creative and efficient means of digital communication that is supported by "cut/copy and paste" techniques (2012, 65). Karyn Recollet's (2016) definition of remixing features performances that are actuated within Indigenous new media platforms. Martin Irvine offers that *generative dialogic principles* for the remix are constituted in "ongoing dialogic chains and networks" (2014, 16). Conceptually, TVC remixing involves altering or changing preexisting materials and the practice of "refunctioning, by societal 'outsiders,' of artifacts and symbols associated with the dominant culture" (Dery 1994, 185). The latter description best supports the theoretical, computational, and generative aspects of remixing, which sets the stage for other TVC modes of production and STEAM activities explored in other chapters.

Remixing, in practice, means to fiddle and tinker and, by extension, make creative and resourceful use of whatever materials are at hand, building things through trial and error. These techniques transcend the Western practice of bricolage (see Lévi-Strauss 1962) and belie the view that nondominant artists and practitioners use only simplistic technologies: remixing requires sophistication and a mastery of materials. Artists remix to amplify their meanings, which often involves adapting materials from different sources. For example, artists remix to apply the geometry in cultural designs to other materials, such as fabric and metal.

Sanford Biggers's "Lotus" design (discussed in chapter 4) is a remix of a blossoming lotus flower. Proximity to the image allows a different type of investigation. Inside each petal shape is a repeating pattern of slave bodies lined in rows in the hold of a ship. Biggers also remixed the Buddhist mandala, transforming it into a hip-hop break dancing cypher to amplify a cultural practice that engages performers and audiences. The hip-hop rap cypher, which took place in the Boston Arts Academy STEAM Lab (see figure 3.1), follows a similar circular arrangement with students taking turns with

Figure 3.1
A meeting of the Freestyle Rap Club in the STEAM Lab at Boston Arts Academy, 2015. Photo: Nettrice Gaskins. Courtesy of Boston Arts Academy.

a microphone, remixing digital media, and interacting with electronic sound interfaces that they created.

As a form of discourse, the remix acts as a cultural binder bringing elements together (Navas 2012). It relies on the relentless combination of all things possible and therefore is a conduit for future imaginary relationships (Recollet 2016). Whereas creativity unleashes the potential of existing ideas, artifacts, and systems, remixing inspires innovation by taking what already exists and improving on it. The remix takes on any shape and medium, providing openings for new applications, modes of production, and technological platforms. Remixing validates cultural practices by drawing on generational influences to tell stories in multimodal contexts. For example, the artist Stephanie Dinkins uses machine learning—a form of artificial intelligence—to train machines to create stories. Dinkins's "Not the Only One," or N'TOO, machine repurposes and remixes text from Toni Morrison's novel *Sula* and the artist's family interviews to respond to questions.

Remixing reflects a broad cultural shift spurred by the internet and is a source of enormous creative potential for digital and online applications (Eglash et al. 2006; Bennett 2016; Dasgupta et al. 2016). Through remixing, artists can collage or layer artifacts or cut, paste, or stack objects. Computers can be used to simulate the remixing process by manipulating 2D bitmap (digital) blocks with code. Remixing though *computational thinking*—problem-solving using computers—and digital fabrication can lead to the creation of physical and digital artifacts that are part of an individual's or group's legacy.

Remixing Heritage: From Artifacts to Algorithms

"Heritage" refers to aspects of culture that are passed along from one generation to next, to be preserved for the future. TVC remixing facilitates a process of reimagining heritage—practitioners remix artifacts from tangible culture, such as art and crafts, with intangible culture, such as folklore, traditions and language, natural elements, and technology. These *heritage artifacts* can, as noted by Audrey Bennett (2016), recirculate as a form of computational agency in STEAM education. Works by Indigenous artists demonstrate a vision of the future that, according to Recollet, is "attentive to the past as it critiques the present, and ventures forward into the beyond" (2016, 91). In other cultures, heritage artifacts such as cosmograms represent temporal and spatial elements that work in tandem with technology (Gaskins 2016).

Chilean-born Guillermo Bert uses digital fabrication to create objects embedded with bar codes that remix and extend the iconography of heritage artifacts such as Chilean textiles that are encoded with culturally specific designs. The Haudenosaunee (Iroquois) artist and technologist Amelia Winger-Bearskin remixes stories with heritage artifacts such as the wampum shell bead of the Eastern Woodlands tribes. Winger-Bearskin (2018) writes that the ready-made features of an existing cultural object, used on an accessible platform with tools that everyone has, enables anyone to participate in the telling of a story. Vancouver-based Skookum Sound System remixes through "glyphing," combining ancient petroglyph rock carvings with hip-hop graffiti tagging and break dancing.

Native American star quilt designs have been remixed by African American quilters whose works reflect the algorithmic nature of the quilting process: the craftsperson follows a series of steps to form a geometric pattern with pieces of fabric sometimes referred to as blocks or modules. The blocks are often rearranged by visual artists to create new designs. Heritage artifacts such as star quilts, urban graffiti, and African cornrow hair braiding has, according to Audrey Bennett (2016), underused computational potential. The *algorithmic designs* embedded in these heritage artifacts link traditional craft making with computational thinking, coding, and the use of machines for fabrication such as 3D printers and laser cutters.

From Computational Thinking to Computational Action

"Computational thinking" (CT) refers to problem-solving methods such as decomposition, pattern recognition, and abstraction that express solutions as computational steps, or algorithms, that can be carried out by computers. CT came out of a need to effectively teach computer literacy in K–12 education (see Papert 1980) and has emerged as a fundamental skill (Wing 2016). However, researchers argue that to be effective CT needs to be situated in real-world contexts (Tissenbaum, Sheldon, and Abelson 2019). *Computational action* advocates argue that learners need to create with code in ways that are relevant to their everyday lives. TVC remixing reduces barriers to putting computational action into practice by demonstrating how cultural artifacts are open to CT problem-solving methods. TVC remixing is computational when practitioners make use of computational principles like algorithmic design—problem-solving using ordered steps.

TVC computational remixing uses *heritage algorithms* that are amenable to algorithmic design (Bennett 2016). Ron Eglash (Eglash and Garvey 2014) and Shirin Vossoughi (Vossoughi, Hooper, and Escudé 2016) study the connection between culture and computation to broaden the definition of "information technology" and to show how computation in certain cultural practices counters cybernetic Western histories as a way to reconstruct identity, social position, and access to power. Equity questions such as *who* gets to create these algorithms and *what* they can do with them face teachers who are tasked with helping their students learn how to code. A multinational study has shown that students who know the basic syntax of coding—rules that define a programming language—are often unable to apply this knowledge to solve real problems (Lister et al. 2005). Teaching STEAM with heritage algorithms leads to a more equitable environment for student groups that are not just underrepresented in STEAM but also marginalized in computer science.

Through TVC remixing, the algorithm for the rhythmic patterns in James Brown's "Cold Sweat" allows sequential elements to be manipulated to create new work. Snead describes the song's basic pattern as A-B-C-B-A, with each new pattern set off by a random response (to the basic pattern), also referred to as "the cut" (1990, 221). Web-based "Morning O" by Zimbabwe-born, US-based artist Nontsikelelo Mutiti plays the transcript of a hair-braiding session. The program creates a braided pattern in the spaces between sentences. This pattern simulates the braiding process, which includes mapping and parting a customer's hair before plaiting cornrows (figure 3.2). "Cold Sweat" and "Morning O" provide different approaches to CT and computational action, using algorithmic calculations to manipulate rhythmic patterns sonically and visually while repurposing and remixing heritage artifacts.

Guillermo Bert's "La Bestia" interactive storytelling tapestry, a collaboration with a community of Mayan weavers in Guatemala,

Figure 3.2
"Ruka (To Braid, to Knit, to Weave)" by Nontsikelelo Mutiti at Recess in New York City in 2014.
Photo: Nettrice Gaskins. Courtesy of the artist.

features a freight train that crosses Mexico to the US-Mexico border (figure 3.3). The quick response (QR) code, a type of 2D bar code read by mobile devices, is embedded in the piece to trigger a video interview with a migrant; the code was created using the artist's innovative laser-etching technique. Amelia Winger-Bearskin writes about how the stories we tell today are embedded in networks and pixels, "for the people I do not yet know, and those I have only met in dreams" (2018). Winger-Bearskin's "Wampum" remixes the shell beads used by Eastern Woodlands nations as a ceremonial pledge with code (figure 3.4). Wampum, as a unit of Indigenous exchange, functions much as a modern-day blockchain transaction.

Projects like "La Bestia," and "Wampum" use heritage algorithms to remix sequences, units, blocks, and modules in the process of creation. "Wampum" and "Morning O" constantly grow as new sequences of recordings are added to them. "La Bestia" and "Cold Sweat" illuminate alternative forms of narrative through the remixing of visual and sonic patterns. "Cold Sweat" was used as an example of a basis for computational remixing, but it also demonstrates embodied improvisation, which is explored in chapters 5 and 6. The song shows the computational aspects of music production that include statements with sounds that are played x number of times to trigger sequences that can be looped repeatedly (figure 3.5). The rhythmic patterns in "Cold Sweat" can be visualized using software, projected two dimensionally on walls, and translated into 3D models for sculpture or architectural projects.

Heritage algorithms are amplified in *Afrofuturism* (further defined in the introduction), which emphasizes a culturally sustaining orientation to technology as a resource for liberatory creativity and improvisation and extends humanity into new realms through technology. The orientation of Afrofuturism in computational disciplines makes it a rich resource for creative expression through TVC remixing and STEAM integration. For example, Hyphen Labs' "NeuroSpeculative AfroFeminism," or NSAF, is an Afrofuturistic

Figure 3.3
"La Bestia" by Guillermo Bert.
Photo: Guillermo Bert. Courtesy of the artist.

Figure 3.4
"Wampum" by Amelia Winger-Bearskin.
Photo: Amelia Winger-Bearskin. Courtesy of the artist.

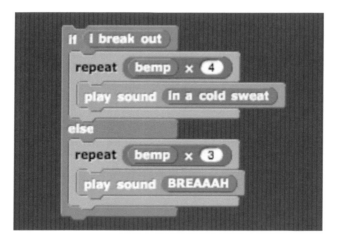

Figure 3.5
The funk song "Cold Sweat" by James Brown and Pee Wee Ellis as an algorithm.
Photo: Nettrice Gaskins.

cross-platform project that remixes the concept of a hair salon through product design, virtual reality, and scientific research addressing real-world issues faced by women of color (Weber 2018).

Afrofuturity, as a making process, engages individuals and communities in collaborative problem-solving, the reimagining and rearranging of time and space through speculative design, fabrication, and performance. Remixing facilitates these practitioners responding to problems with novel ideas and concepts that involve building blocks of cultural heritage, computational tools, and making processes. The projects highlighted in this chapter show an emerging strategy that positions practitioners from diverse backgrounds as creative generators who use remixing to create artifacts of value for their communities and the world.

Remixing through Culturally Relevant Making

The maker movement merged digital technologies with more traditional DIY artisan practices, forming a culture that values tinkering, iterative prototyping, and invention. Emerging research has begun to challenge leaders in the maker movement to consider new directions that include expanding what counts as making (Calabrese Barton and Tan 2018; Kafai, Fields, and Searle 2014), as well as programs and pedagogies that support an equitable culture of making and incorporate participants' cultural knowledge and practices (Calabrese Barton and Tan 2018; Tucker-Raymond et al. 2016). The culturally relevant aspects of making, especially as it relates to TVC remixing, have yet to be explored in depth, and maker practices still tend to be grounded in gendered, white, middle-class culture.

Scholars distinguish makers from nondominant groups whose works confront "normative understandings" of STEAM ingenuity (Vossoughi, Hooper, and Escudé 2016, 207), questioning who is viewed as an inventor, creator, or maker and who makes the terms by which the work is valued. Remixing with heritage artifacts and algorithms demonstrate the breadth and depth of culturally relevant maker practices and the ways these practices can be meaningfully connected to STEAM concepts (Schwartz and Gutiérrez 2015).

Culturally situated design tools (CSDTs) leverage the underused computational potential in cultural artifacts such as ideograms, quilts, and cornrow hair braiding to help people learn math and computation (Bennett 2016). Computational remixing tools like these have been associated with increased likelihood of using coding to find solutions to problems (Dasgupta et al. 2016). Many CSDTs take advantage of visual programming platforms (VPLs) and their visual blocks of code to do computer programming. In a VPL students can remix these blocks to generate musical sequences, braid segments, and textile blocks, which can then be digitally fabricated through 3D printing, laser cutting, and physical computing (electronics). (See figures 3.6 and 3.7.)

Heritage algorithms, like some VPLs, are characterized by their *modularity*, which means that different components can be separated and recombined, often with the benefits of flexibility and variety in use. TVC remixing using VPLs can play a role in facilitating and sustaining purposeful engagement by nurturing traditional artistic practices and by creating paths to learning (Bennett 2016). To do this work, software developers should understand how the original cultural designs such as fractals in African architecture and iterative patterns in Native American weaving are made. For example, developers at Rensselaer Polytechnic Institute collaborated with artists to craft CSDTs that demonstrate how to generate cultural designs based on the artists' works. In turn, the artists can incorporate the computational designs in their physical work, demonstrating what is called a *design loop* (Rodriguez 2014).

The computational design loop functions as a design cypher, engaging value generators (artists) and developers in tasks that culminate in making new work. Nontsikelelo Mutiti remixes

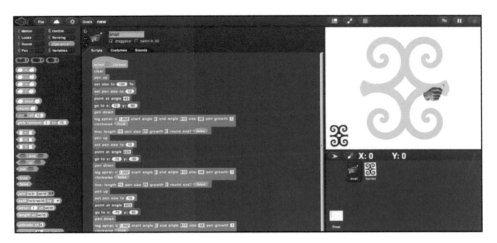

Figure 3.6
Computational remixing using the Adinkra CSDT.
Photo: Nettrice Gaskins.

Figure 3.7
3D printed design from the Adinkra CSDT.
Photo: Nettrice Gaskins.

cornrow-inspired tile patterns to generate designs, an inquiry into "rule-based image making, graphic aesthetic with mathematics at the foundation" (Adebayo 2017). She situates braiding within the realm of computation by means of *ruka*, which in the Shona language describes braiding, weaving, and knitting. Rensselaer worked with Mutiti to develop the Ruka CSDT, which repeatedly stamps tile motifs based on geometry (rotation, reflection, translation) to make new patterns (figure 3.8). The Ruka CSDT can also be used to generate patterns like those displayed by Ghanaian Kente cloth.

TVC practitioners incorporate aspects of remixing in their visually rhythmic designs to achieve uniqueness. Something similar happens rhythmically in music, specifically in the genres jazz, rap, and funk (Wahlman 2001). The semisymmetry in African weaving and African American quilt making are achieved by the juxtaposition of distinct geometric motifs and by controlled variations in texture, scale, shape, orientation, or color. The algorithms that generate these cultural heritage designs are also referred to as shape grammars

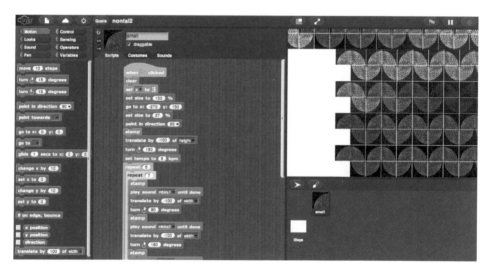

Figure 3.8
The Ruka CSDT based on art by Nontsikelelo Mutiti.
Photo: Nettrice Gaskins. Courtesy of Rensselaer Polytechnic Institute.

(discussed in chapter 1), or rules that define how a module such as a tile or block can be transformed. Through remixing, practitioners use their own rules and procedures for constructing cultural artifacts based on their knowledge and experiences.

Computation (making) grammars involve *doing* and *seeing* with elements that create shapes (Knight and Stiny 2015). Mutiti's Ruka makes use of discrete modules that can be changed, assembled, or reassembled using different operations and transformations. These modules are amenable to remixing. Ruka involves doing and seeing: actions such as making tiles to print designs on and looking where to place or move a braid tile to create a design. The Ruka CSDT simulates this process, linking computation and making to cultural production. This VPL-based CSDT is part of a suite of tools that simulate remixing and artistic processes such as printmaking and floor installation.

Incorporating CSDTs like Ruka into maker education can expand the definition of what making is and who gets to be a maker. Students learn how computation connects to familiar activities like braiding, weaving, and tagging. Heritage artifacts simulated using digital tools such as VPLs and computational rhetoric acknowledge students' cultural identities, showing them that they have the capacity to develop computational products that have authentic impact in their lives.

4

Remixing in Teaching and Learning

Eight Latino/a and Indigenous high school–age interns met graduate digital media students near the Wells Park Community Project in Albuquerque, New Mexico, to create an interactive outdoor mural. They joined in a design cypher that was part of a STEMarts workshop during which participants took inspiration from Indigenous cultural artifacts, contemporary artworks, and the natural world. The workshop challenged participants to repurpose and combine these artifacts and images to develop an overall mural design. They used mobile augmented reality (AR)—the layering of digital artifacts over physical objects—to connect cultural artifacts to the youths' daily lives; used software to explore the mathematical concepts embodied in the designs; and used mural painting methods that scaled elements without changing the proportions.

Participants came up with the theme Life and Death, which provided a focus for the mural. The final composition showed unity within duality: life and death may appear to be in opposition, but they were seen by the participants as integral parts of a larger whole. This idea was conveyed in the performance piece "Myth and Infrastructure" by Miwa Matreyek, which combined images of day and night, superimposing imagery of the daytime over the night sky. Matreyek's work inspired participants to collage images of New Mexico, and later they added repeating spatial patterns, Mimbres pottery, and tattoo motifs. The use of remixing and computation enhanced and encouraged STEAM learning and provided a model for engaging Indigenous and Latino/a youth in creative problem-solving and art making.

TVC remixing added another dimension to the three-week STEMarts workshop that taught youth how to encode (convert), rearrange, and combine (collage) heritage artifacts, urban art, and AR. The ideation phase with the high school students, who were interns at the ¡Explora! science museum, included a *design cypher* that mapped meaning to heritage artifacts and visually displayed design concepts and the relationships among those concepts (figure 4.1). Participants used Graffiti Grapher, a culturally situated design tool (CSDT) that simulates graffiti tagging on the basis of Cartesian and polar coordinate geometry. Users mapped their graffiti designs onto these coordinate systems. With the goal of addressing a theme, the interns' next step was to remix and combine their designs to create an AR-enhanced physical mural for community members with camera-enabled mobile devices such as phones, iPads, and tablet computers.

During the first week, the interns were led though a participatory, mural-making process in which they combined ancient Mimbres pottery designs with other designs. The interns were given paper to trace artifacts that were of interest to them. Layering what they drew on tracing paper helped them combine different ideas and create designs (figure 4.2). The facilitators combined the interns' drawings and Graffiti Grapher designs to make one composition, and a grid method was used to enlarge the final image to scale on the outside wall of a building in the Wells Park neighborhood. At the end

Figure 4.1
The Augmented Reality in Open Spaces (AROS) design cypher at the ¡Explora! science museum in Albuquerque, New Mexico.
Photo: Nettrice Gaskins.

of the first week, the interns were split into two groups, with one group learning how to make a mural and the other learning how to create AR content. After the second week, the two groups switched. As a final step, black-and-white AR frame markers (similar to QR codes) were added to the mural (figure 4.3).

In recorded peer interviews, workshop facilitators noted how participants derived different lessons from the instructional materials and found ways to explore their personal interests while working on the same project. For example, Junior, a self-professed graffiti artist, was the first of the interns to figure out how to use the Graffiti Grapher CSDT. In addition to learning how to use the CSDT, Stephanie used tracing paper to replicate repeating-pattern designs and animal drawings she found painted on Mimbres pottery. Christian was attracted to a particular animal:

Figure 4.2
¡Explora! interns learn how to use the scalable, modular mural design process during week one of the AROS workshop.
Photo: Nettrice Gaskins.

Figure 4.3
The final AROS mural at Wells Park in Albuquerque.
Photo: Nettrice Gaskins.

Christian: I found this Mimbres drawing of a bat, so I decided to do my own spin-off of it. . . . I chose the bat because I wanted [my design] to be more symmetrical. For the background I was thinking of using this [*shows Isaiah a different Mimbres design*].

Isaiah: You should try it, Christian. That would look real nice.

What Christian describes here arrives at the purpose of the design mapping exercise that encourages participants to construct new knowledge and make things that are meaningful to them. Through this meaning-making activity, participants explore the similarities and differences between cultural artifacts, contemporary and urban art, and the AR spatial tagging of digital artifacts. They can also explore coordinate geometry and computation when recreating and scaling up the preexisting designs.

Tagging is also expressed through social media behaviors and physical movement such as Indigenous spatial *glyphing* (see Recollet 2016), which captures the urban ambience of graffiti. Glyphing requires knowledge of technology as well as of Indigenous cultural practices and hip-hop aesthetics, so it provides learners with diverse repertoires of practice and adaptive expertise. Glyphing, similar to AR, requires mapping, layering, and tagging with digital artifacts. Tagging is part of *#HipHopEd* pedagogy (see Emdin and Adjapong 2018), which encourages students to make keen observations, ask deep questions, use analytical skills, exhibit curiosity, and provide evidence to show what they have learned from their analyses. Evidence could be in the form of a public art installation, a mobile app, or a live performance.

Computational actions such as graffiti graphing using a CSDT, spatial tagging in AR, and glyphing are *rhetorical performances* (Banks 2011, 14–15) that give learners agency in TVC remixing and in *universal construction environments* (Blikstein 2008, 208) that produce model learning spaces that emphasize the ubiquity of computational making practices that already exist in students' everyday lives.

At ¡Explora! the Latino/a and Indigenous youth worked "in the scratch" by remixing culturally relevant content using digital tools (see Banks 2011, 119), which is similar to messing around, or a transitional mode of participation that mediates between hanging out and being more intensely engaged with technology (Itō, Baumer, and Bittanti 2019).

TVC remixing using computer-based tools helps learners become digitally literate and fosters computational action (Tissenbaum, Sheldon, and Abelson 2019; Kafai and Burke 2016). The use of the CSDT and AR software engaged the ¡Explora! interns with different skills, knowledge, and experiences, and this engagement promotes learning (Dasgupta et al. 2016). Constructionism articulates a theoretical foundation for computational tools and AR applications in maker education by allowing users to overlay, combine, and rearrange 2D and 3D artifacts in a physical space (Roussos et al. 1997). By combining culturally relevant content with computational action, ¡Explora! youth learned how remixing and making things using technology can be a part of their everyday lives.

Building on the AROS Workshop Model

The STEMarts workshop at ¡Explora! led to the development of a TVC design and culturally relevant making approach that works with constructionist strategies, specifically because students get to work on projects that connect what they know with new knowledge from teachers, artists, and other experts who draw on diverse repertoires of practice such as remixing and computational action to create their work. The approach includes differentiated instruction and design cyphers that help learners acquire knowledge, skills, or dispositions that enable them to act, think, and feel in ways that are recognized as important for themselves and their communities. This approach also informed future workshops and classes that applied TVC remixing to attract students to project-based STEAM learning activities.

In 2012, a formal study (see Gaskins 2014) was launched at Drew Charter School (DCS) in southeast Atlanta, Georgia, to investigate project-based STEAM learning using materials and methods from the Augmented Reality in Open Spaces (AROS) workshop. The DCS study examined how TVC practices such as remixing could deepen STEAM learning and explored heritage artifacts, mathematics, and computation. Two hundred fourth- and eighth-grade students were recruited to participate in the STEAM workshops. These workshops provided participants with resources and opportunities for learning by doing using the concept of *modularity* to create a richer, more multifaceted learning experience for students than conventional approaches.

Modularity aids in the remixing of existing content and materials. For example, elements can be layered to produce a collage, and blocks or motifs can be rearranged to demonstrate students' knowledge of mathematics. Students can simulate arts and crafts by moving blocks around with designs on them to show geometric transformations such as rotation, translation, and reflection. Using CSDTs, students remix blocks of code to produce new designs. The use of learning modules also helps in the creation of materials and tools that help teachers across grade levels create activities that demonstrate their students' understanding and knowledge of computational action, STEAM concepts, and creative practices (or performances).

DCS activities included mapping, or creating diagrammatic representations of an area or a concept and the manipulation of existing design motifs on paper and with CSDTs to create designs. Students learned about African American quilts and work by contemporary artists that reuses artifacts such as quilts or maps and how these examples demonstrate concepts in mathematics and computation. DCS students learned about quilts being used as maps in the Underground Railroad and how artists remix or reuse the quilts. The instructional materials and digital tools were used to simulate arti-facts and encourage TVC remixing to create STEAM projects.

For the DCS study, one class of fourth-grade students was given paper quilt templates that they cut into squares, or blocks. They were instructed to move the blocks around, similar to the way African American quilt makers rearrange fabric blocks. The students also used the Biggers CSDT to simulate a pattern based on Sanford Biggers's "Lotus" design, mentioned in chapter 3, and learned how the artist mapped meaning to the motif (figure 4.4).

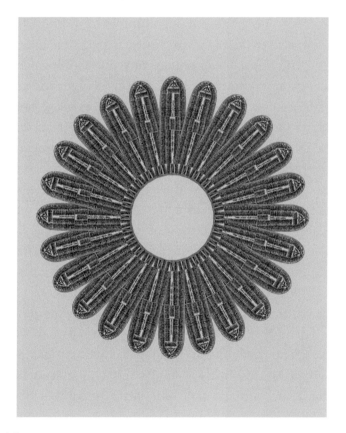

Figure 4.4
"Lotus" by Sanford Biggers.
Photo and credit: Courtesy of the artist.

Analysis of "Lotus" was done through *close looking*, or engaging carefully with the artifact in a meaningful and personal manner. After students learned that the lotus flower is a divine symbol in Buddhist and Hindu traditions, they were shown how to import and animate a petal shape (from the artist's rendition). The close-looking activity with students (see Gaskins 2014) began as follows:

Facilitator: What do you see?

Students: A flower; a sun; petals.

Facilitator: What is inside of the petals?

Students: Fingers, arrows . . . what is it?

Facilitator (after a short pause): It is a slave ship.

Student 1: Oh!

Facilitator: What does it mean? Why did he combine two images together?

Students: Peace, freedom for slaves, beautiful . . .

By closely analyzing the "Lotus" image, DCS students were able to identify concepts that had personal meaning to them. This activity sets the stage for further experimentation and play with digital tools. Close looking can activate a student's curiosity, which can be a powerful motivator of behavior, initiating actions directed at exploring the environment to resolve uncertainty and make new concepts and ideas more familiar (Arnone et al. 2011). When students look more closely at something, they may see things that trigger questions. However, close looking does not automatically progress to higher levels of engagement, greater learning, or mastery. Students need opportunities to design and make projects using what they have learned. Tools and methods also need to be created to assess STEAM learning.

After learning about the meaning of "Lotus" the students practiced remixing using the Romare Bearden Remixes application on their iPads. The app allows users to remix works from the artist and create new versions, as an expression of their personal journey. They can select from a variety of backdrops, rearrange and collage (layer) shapes and designs taken from Bearden's art, cut out their own shapes, and add or change other elements.

A different DCS fourth-grade class practiced remixing and meaning making by exploring a process used by Ethiopian American artist Julie Mehretu, who remixes aerial maps in her paintings. After closely analyzing Mehretu's work, students learned how to find and print out Google Earth maps of their neighborhoods. They used a method called *personal meaning mapping* (PMM) to add and combine layers of tags—text, symbols, shapes—on semitransparent tracing paper (figure 4.5). Clear plastic sheets were used for additional tags.

Mapping helps document the remixing process, as well as foster alternative formative assessments within STEAM and maker

Figure 4.5
Fourth-grade DCS students make personal meaning maps by layering and drawing on tracing paper at DCS in Atlanta, Georgia.
Photo: Nettrice Gaskins. Courtesy of Drew Charter School.

education contexts. PMMs—derived from concept mapping (see Daley 2004; Falk 2003)—capture student engagement with instructional materials and foster the students' exploration of relevant concepts. The DCS students' PMMs were analyzed along four semi-independent dimensions: extent, breadth, depth, and mastery (Falk and Storksdieck 2005). Breadth measures the number of conceptual categories each student uses to describe a prompt. If the prompt is "Write or draw as many words/things you can think of to describe your neighborhood," then breadth measures the several ways that "neighborhood" can be understood, as students use layers to contextualize the prompt. For depth, students created tags in additional layers, especially to represent math principles in their designs.

Developing the TVC Design Tool Kit

After the study at DCS concluded, another STEAM workshop took place at a nearby middle school in Lithonia, Georgia. The workshop introduced Lithonia Middle School (LMS) students to computational (shape) grammars (Knight and Stiny 2015) and set the stage for further experimentation and play with digital tools. LMS students were provided with paper quilt templates to remix and create patterns inspired by African American quilts (figure 4.6). They used CSDTs to simulate designs by Afrofuturist artists (figure 4.7). Remixing elements such as quilt blocks and other cultural artifacts addresses personal, situational, and contextual factors that support student autonomy and competence, as well as engenders active, deep learning. These culturally relevant tools, methods, and materials are part of a TVC design tool kit to teach students how to solve problems using different artifacts and create their own designs.

As part of the STEAM workshop, LMS teachers and students visited Georgia Tech's Robert C. Williams Museum of Papermaking

Figure 4.6
A sixth-grade student uses a paper template to remix quilt-based motifs and make her own design at Lithonia Middle School in Lithonia, Georgia.
Photo: Nettrice Gaskins. Courtesy of Lithonia Middle School.

where they learned about colonial maps of Africa and vernacular mapping—mapping with cultural information—including a traditional (heritage) African map that is read by touching its surface. Lukasa personal memory maps are devices used by practitioners in the oral retelling of history in Luba culture from the African Congo (see figure 4.8). At the museum, LMS students also explored an interactive tabletop lukasa that transforms users' personal histories into projected animations.

Mapping with heritage artifacts like the physical and digital lukasa show the formal possibilities of geometric variation, which align with the mathematics principles of rotation, reflection, translation, dilation, and more. Looking at these principles through the lens of vernacular mapping and heritage develops a methodology

Figure 4.7
Students use an Afrofuturism CSDT to simulate artwork by Saya Woolfalk at Lithonia Middle School in Lithonia, Georgia.
Photo: Nettrice Gaskins. Courtesy of Lithonia Middle School.

for engaging aspects of culturally relevant making and computational remixing that builds on students' STEAM capital and characteristics of interest and motivation. This approach challenges educators to locate analogies between the artifacts or models and STEAM subjects they need to teach.

Formative and summative assessments for the STEAM workshops were developed on the basis of specific cultural contexts and the shared practices of underrepresented ethnic groups. The results of the LMS workshop suggest that the use of TVC remixing and digital tools inside and outside of the classroom can enhance the degree to which students can show their understanding of STEAM concepts. To assess the value of the workshop, students received an Instructional Materials Motivation Survey, which measures levels of interest using the Attention, Relevance, Confidence, and Satisfaction (ARCS) model of motivation (Keller 2010). The results of this study

Figure 4.8
Lithonia Middle School students at the Robert C. Williams Museum of Papermaking
learning about lukasa memory boards from Professor Kenneth Knoespel.
Photo: Nettrice Gaskins. Courtesy of Georgia Tech.

concluded that remixing through vision and personal meaning
mapping, and the use of digital tools, increased student interest and
personal motivation (Gaskins 2014).

The use of digital tools to remix heritage artifacts reveals how
cultural technologies can be used to recognize other ways of knowing, learning, and making, creating a more inclusive learning environment where students can explore different ideas with intense
personal engagement (Blikstein 2013, 207). Cultural artifacts (e.g.,
maps, cosmograms, and lukasa), interactive interfaces and devices,
and CSDTs are part of a TVC design tool kit and framework for
STEAM learning that circulates "value in the arts back to underrepresented ethnic communities" (Bennett 2016, 588). This approach
is in contrast to the historical practice of extracting cultural capital
from these communities without recognition or compensation.

Ethnocomputational Creativity in STEAM

Examples of *ethnocomputational creativity*—the use of computation to circulate value—can be found in Marvel's film *Black Panther*. The film's set and costume designers embedded heritage artifacts such as Adinkra and African-lace patterns into costumes and props and digitally manufactured objects like hats and shoulder mantles worn by the actors (McIntyre 2018). Projects that combine heritage artifacts and algorithmic designs give students access to a range of digital manufacturing technologies and knowledge. The process used for *Black Panther* can be adapted for STEAM learning by simulating designs in the film using CSDTs, then output in file formats for digital fabrication using a laser cutter or 3D printer.

Ethnocomputational creativity can also happen in physical computing that involves assembling and connecting electronic components that sense and respond to the environment. Multitouch systems such as touch tables enable multiple users to concurrently make contact with a surface. For example, at the Papermaking museum, LMS students used a digital lukasa touch table to touch, interact with, and remix physical and digital artifacts (figure 4.9). The table demonstrates how emerging digital-media-interaction technologies are used to revisit the way non-Western cultures map the world using tangible, embodied, and performative methods (Ho Chu et al. 2015; Mazalek and Clifton 2014).

Having access to CSDTs and other tools such as the digital lukasa touch table led to more active student engagement in the STEAM workshop. LMS students remixed tangible shell objects on the touch table, and this helped reinforce their personal and sociocultural learning. These physical objects have QR codes (a 2D bar code) printed on them that trigger animations. This technology is similar to other types of markers used in AR applications. QR and AR code elements can be painted on walls (murals) or woven into heritage artifacts and tapestries, as demonstrated by Guillermo Bert's "La Bestia," mentioned in chapter 3.

Figure 4.9
LMS students explore the digital lukasa table at the Museum of Papermaking in Atlanta, Georgia.
Photo: Nettrice Gaskins. Courtesy of Georgia Tech.

One important takeaway from this chapter is that TVC remixing activities can value students' experiences, cultures, and communities by leveraging them as learning platforms for content and pedagogy. TVC remixing involves various sources that teach students about cultural heritage, and the process can help students better understand the cultural context of STEAM and making. TVC remixing can help educators adapt data-collection instruments such as personal meaning maps and instructional materials surveys that ensure appropriateness for underrepresented ethnic groups on the basis of the cultural practices of the groups. Remixing shows how underrepresented ethnic students can be engaged in STEAM through sharing, exchanging, and generating information that is of value to the students and their communities.

III   Improvisation

5
Tangible and Embodied Improvisation

This chapter addresses *improvisation*—the spontaneous and inventive use of materials—which is a critical element of TVC. Improvisation, as a cultural practice, elicits the active engagement or participation of underrepresented ethnic communities. TVC improvisation, as a critical pedagogy, builds on improvisation scholarship and looks at how practitioners use cultural designs and heritage artifacts—objects with computational potential—to embody time, space, and technology. The chapter looks at theories by Christopher Andreae (2004), James A. Snead (1990), and Geneva Smitherman (1977, 2000) and connects their work with research on technologies that align with embodiment (El-Zanfaly 2015; Kaufman and Beghetto 2019), making grammars and craft performances (Knight 2018; Knight and Stiny 2015), and fabrication (Wood 2015; Bales 2012; Wahlman 2001).

Improvisation as a form of research is another way of thinking that produces ideas that are dynamic, spontaneous, and ever changing (De Spain 2003, 7). Improvisations stage the emergence of new forms and practices in which one moves from event to event, decision to decision, and retrospectively creates connections only to dissolve them again. Improvisations create a desire for continuation and open up possibilities for action. Improvisation is described as a "computation of complex forms that produce and reproduce, building complexity and relating structured and unstructured, prepared and unprepared, known and unknown elements to each other" (Landgraf 2014, 147). An improvisational work responds to itself, repeats, alters, and rephrases what has come before.

Improvisation in cultural production emphasizes the call-and-response participatory aspect of jazz, funk, and other creative forms that include polyrhythms and the repetition of motifs with variation. Call-and-response is a key manner of doing improvisation in diasporic African cultural production (Snead 1990) and Indigenous performances (McCluskey 1995). TVC improvisation compares to research that situates embodied interaction between performers and artifacts and to the computational making processes generated during the creation of traditional art and crafts. This includes the direct physical and temporal qualities of making and the use of hardware and software to generate and transmit data to devices, trigger sounds, and control parameters of electronic performances.

This chapter explores works that demonstrate how TVC improvisation applies critical theory to STEAM and making. The examples in this chapter are of TVC improvisation used by practitioners to correlate multisensory input with their bodily experiences using elaborate feedback mechanisms to guide their actions (Iyer 2002). TVC improvisation has the capacity to *synthesize*, or see relationships between seemingly unrelated concepts and subjects. For example, Sanford Biggers, who was mentioned previously, made visible the hip-hop ritual of the break dance cypher that consists of acrobatic transitions and, finally, an exit that returns the dancer to the outside of the circle (George et al. 1985, 90).

Embodied Improvisation with Heritage Artifacts

TVC improvisation is embodied and makes use of artifacts that are deeply rooted in diasporic and Indigenous structures and traditions.

For example, the cosmogram is a geometric figure that goes by other names in different cultures. Each cosmographic design has its own purpose and meaning. In the Americas it is called the Medicine Wheel or Sacred Hoop and embodies the four directions, as well as Father Sky, Mother Earth, and Spirit Tree—all of which symbolize dimensions of health and the cycles of life. Powwows and related Indigenous cultural traditions bring communities together through circle or round dancing where the drum, audience, and judges form one circle and the remaining encampment forms another circle, with performances in the center (McCluskey 1995). Call-and-response in powwows involve a change of direction.

The Fist & Heel Performance Group engages audiences in call-and-response participation, especially in "Moses(es)," a dance performance that centers the *ring shout*, an ecstatic and transcendent religious ritual first practiced by enslaved African people in the West Indies and the United States, in which worshipers move counterclockwise in a circle while moving their feet and clapping their hands (see Juba in the introduction). The ring shout is an example of performers embodying the circular design of the cosmogram. The recursive elements of the performance can be found in fractal geometry and computation. Fractals are created through a circular process, as an iterative feedback loop (Eglash 1999, 17).

The ring shout embodies the design of the Kongo Cosmogram from West Central Africa (figure 5.1), which visualizes ritual and movement, as well as spaces of transformation. This circular design has resonance, from the ring shout and powwow to other formations such as hip-hop cyphers. Cosmograms are evident in the designs of Sanford Biggers's previously mentioned "Lotus" piece and his *Mandala of the B-Bodhisattva*, which was initially used as a break dance floor installation for a Battle of the Boroughs competition. Biggers's *Mandala* replicates the circular movement of the cypher, which sustains rhythmic motion, continuity, and circularity via flow (Rose 1994).

TVC practitioners improvise over musical compositions using cyclical rhythm patterns that repeat elements, and a phenomenal

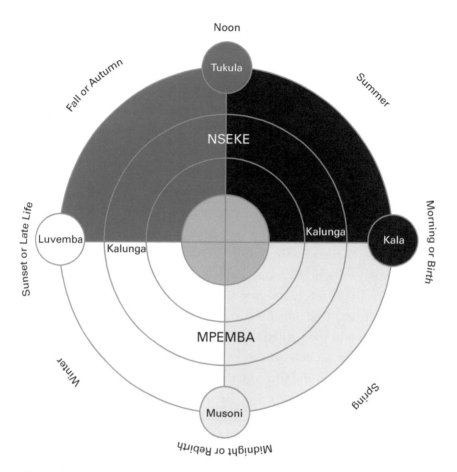

Figure 5.1
A rendition of the Kongo Cosmogram.
Photo: Nettrice Gaskins.

amount of change and development can occur in the process. For example, musicians deliberately fracture and disrupt typical rhythmic patterns to create arrangements. Improvisation through repetition is activated by the use of designs that play out patterns. For the song "Giant Steps," jazz maverick John Coltrane created a way to use a cosmographic design as a mnemonic device (figure 5.2). Coltrane was inspired by quantum mechanics, a physics domain that looks at how objects travel (Alexander 2017). He made a correlation

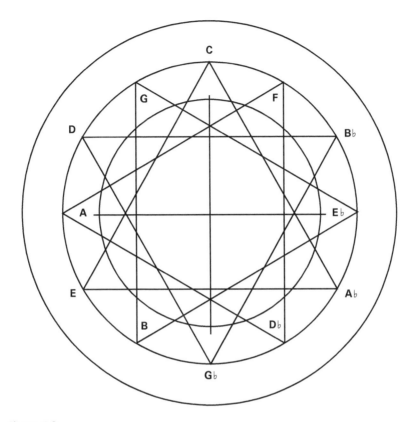

Figure 5.2
A rendition of the mnemonic device John Coltrane created for "Giant Steps."
Photo: Nettrice Gaskins.

to how musicians improvise, playing with all possible notes on a
scale (Rudolph 2010). What Coltrane did with sound is similar to
what artists do with visual designs (figure 5.3).

Embodied improvisation with heritage artifacts is actuated
through repetition (Recollet 2016; Dillon 2012). The repetition in
James Brown's "Cold Sweat" and other songs use algorithms that
generate and disrupt rhythmic patterns, as mentioned in chapter 3.
Rap group Public Enemy used this method when sampling "Cold
Sweat" in "Welcome to the Terrordome," which was later resampled
in A Tribe Called Red's "Stadium Pow Wow." A Tribe Called Red is

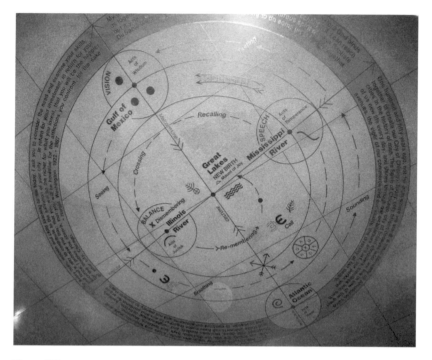

Figure 5.3
DuSable's Journey (1991), by Houston Conwill.
Photo: Nettrice Gaskins. Courtesy of Harold Washington Public Library, Chicago, Illinois.

an Indigenous Canadian DJ collective that is known for blending samples of powwow drumming, singing, and chanting with hip-hop and electronic music called dubstep. Through improvisation, the group uses technology to create dissonance between electronic drumbeats and stereotypical Native sounds—to disrupt offensive behavior such as the *war chant* and the motion of a *tomahawk chop* in US sports culture (Guestlistener 2014).

Hip-hop aesthetics and remixing activate Indigenous spatial glyphing performances (see chapter 4) that show how embodied improvisation disrupts the "colonial organizing of land, bodies, and social and political landscapes" (Goeman 2013, 3). Spatial glyphs are gestures made with the human body; they are used by indigenous practitioners to remix dance and to merge cultural artifacts with hip-hop break dancing. Skookum Sound System's "Ay I Oh Stomp" merges graffiti and spatial tagging with technology (Recollet 2016). The performers' dance poses copy ancient petroglyph engravings. Sacred Hoop dances combine sequential, complex tricks and transitions with the hoop, which represents unity, oneness, wholeness, and infinity.

Navajo artist Bert Benally and Chinese dissident Ai Weiwei collaborated on a site-specific land installation. Benally referenced the cosmogram as a Native American Medicine Wheel; Weiwei, as a bicycle wheel; with both works representing the cultural rituals of their respective communities. "Pull of the Moon" included a live, remote performance that included the use of sound that connected the artists' contributions. An experimental immersive film digitally re-created the remote performance at Coyote Canyon, New Mexico, by using cutting-edge computational techniques such as aerial drone mapping, photogrammetry, and gigapixel panoramic techniques (Villarreal 2014).

Improvisation is a pivotal structural device created by stylistic forms that emphasize certain aesthetic qualities and narratives. The artist Xenobia Bailey, mentioned earlier in this book, takes inspiration from Coltrane when creating crochet cosmograms, consisting of repeating patterns of concentric circles. Thematic variations are prevalent in African American quilting (see Bales 2012; Wahlman 2001), collage, and painting. These works capture what Terry Knight (2018, 206) refers to as the improvisational—sociocultural, temporal, and performative (embodied)—aspects of craft that "provide insights into its creative and generative possibilities." Knight proposes a new computational theory for *making grammars* that points to new possibilities for the use of heritage artifacts in computational craft making.

Embodying Improvisation in Craft Methods

African diasporic stylistic elements such as collective improvisation include controlled or spontaneous feedback, artist, and audience participation and immersion in different language platforms (Ludigkeit 2001, 174). These improvisational techniques are different from those of their European and Western counterparts, using what Snead refers to as the *cut*, which is an "abrupt, seemingly unmotivated break" in an established sequence and the "willed return" to a prior part of a ritual, dance, or beat (1990, 221). Products of this technique include the groove in funk music, cutting and scratching (see chapter 3) with devices to remix sounds, and "African Americanizing" traditional Euro-American quilt patterns (Bales 2012; Wahlman 2001).

These examples show how practitioners perform aesthetic gestures based on preset commands and algorithms. They can respond to a certain sequence or pattern, especially through call-and-response. Funk music usually consists of danceable rhythm sequences that players respond to by disrupting the set arrangements. The funk aesthetic, which is derived from funk music, involves the use of repurposed or sampled elements such as rhythm, melody, speech, and other sounds to improvise with. Hip-hop producers use drum machines and audio samplers to emulate this process. African American quilters improvise by establishing a pattern in one fabric square, then varying it in size, arrangement, and color in successive squares. The result is a transcript or score of the performance.

Improvisational methods such as call-and-response have been investigated by neuroscientists. A Johns Hopkins study looked at the neuroscience of jazz, hip-hop, and improvisation (Castillo 2011; Limb and Braun 2008). Researchers found that musicians and rappers who are engaged with others in spontaneous improvisation show robust activation in the same brain areas traditionally associated with spoken language and syntax. In other words, improvisational conversations take root in the brain as a language. This is apparent in the way that music and craft performers respond to patterns in a song or a quilt. For example, James Brown and Thelonious Monk were known to improvise or play with and over the grooves their bands had previously recorded. This practice became the foundation for later creative production.

The call-and-response aspect of TVC improvisation is embedded in the repetition of motifs, always with variation (Andreae 2004). Technologies that emulate this spontaneous approach include *making grammars*, which build on shape computations mentioned in earlier chapters that are improvisational, perceptual, and action oriented, defined as "*doing* and *sensing* with *stuff* to make things" (Knight and Stiny 2015, 12). Similar to jazz musicians who improvise during performances, craft performers riff on visual patterns in their work, and these performances are seldom planned but follow basic models. For example, Xenobia Bailey's crochet work demonstrates this.

Improvisation in making involves *embodied creativity*, or the spontaneous interaction between makers, the objects being made, and the machines that produce the objects (El-Zanfaly 2015). Like dancing, making is a situated action, always in flux and sometimes unplanned, around technologies that engage creativity. Doing and sensing actions (see Knight 2015) support embodied creativity through human interactivity and how bodies are situated in environments. Technology extends improvisation through the creation of interactive, tangible objects like controllers and sensors for musical performances, for example. These objects push the boundaries of what is real, especially when they represent interactive physical systems that can sense and respond to performers and the world.

Software that acts on sonic and visual patterns demonstrates computational theory (doing and sensing) and can emulate *rhetorical performances* that persuade audiences to respond to what is being presented (Smitherman 2000). This process includes an initial improvisatory phase, characterized by spontaneous generation of novel material, that is followed by making something new. Hip-hop producers emulate this process when using drum machines and samplers to program and output rhythmic sound patterns. Music, when imported into music visualization software, generates visual patterns similar to cosmograms or fractal-based motifs in African textiles and African American quilts (figure 5.4). Jazz musician Sun Ra, who collaborated with Visual Music Systems, helped develop the Outer Space Visual Communicator, or OVC, a light color instrument with an array of sensors that generate music visualizations.

Embodied improvisation involves performing with digital tools and looks at how these technologies should behave while interacting with humans. In a video interview (see B3R3Z1N4 2008), Doze Green, a pioneering b-boy and artist, talks about how arrows are used to make graffiti letters aerodynamic, emulating dance gestures to indicate directional and elemental forces in the environment. The essence of this performance is captured with Graffiti Analysis, a mobile app that allows graffiti artists to create visualizations of their movements (figure 5.5). The app was created using a markup language that stores graffiti motion data such as x and y coordinates and time (Roth 2005; Schultz 2011).

Embodied improvisation is an aesthetic and epistemic act, a form of *bodily poeticizing* that encompasses knowledge that is "intuitive,

Figure 5.4
Music visualization of James Brown's "Cold Sweat."
Photo: Nettrice Gaskins.

Figure 5.5
Example of a digital graffiti tag created with Graffiti Analysis.
Photo: Nettrice Gaskins. Courtesy of Evan Roth.

somatic, affective, and cognitive" (Lockford and Pelias 2004, 431). However, instead of theatrical staging, improvisational activities use digital tools to capture performances as inputs (tags, sounds, motifs), and the outputs are the systems' response to the data. With wearable technology—electronic devices worn on the body—performers can generate data through motion. This development has implications for understanding how performances become digital artifacts and are translated using computer-based and visual programming systems that interact with the environment.

Machine learning—an emerging field in artificial intelligence—can emulate improvisation in art-based systems. The "machine" is a computational model that observes real-world patterns and tries to create a representation of those patterns. For example, Shantell Martin's "Mind the Machine," mentioned in chapter 1, extracts recurring visual elements, rearranges those elements to generate new artwork, and programs a robot to emulate the artist's improvisational style of drawing. In other words, art-based computational systems can take apart elements of artists' work and improvise. Another example of this is the NSynth Super physical interface for the NSynth machine learning algorithm, which can break down repetitive rhythm sequences and create new ways to make music (figure 5.6).

In TVC improvisation, performances are generative, meaning the interactions of the performers can respond to and trigger images, sounds, or other effects. Fictional representations of this type of interaction include Marvel's *Black Panther*, which channels Wakandan technology into devices worn on the body that respond to touch, movement, or changes in the environment. The film's set and costume designers embedded cultural artifacts such as Adinkra symbols and Nsibidi, an ancient Nigerian language system that

Figure 5.6
A version of the NSynth Super box.
Photo: Nettrice Gaskins.

used symbols instead of words or sounds. The movie's production designer, Hannah Beachler, created an entire alphabet for the film based on Nsibidi (see Desowitz 2018), and costumes were textured with these ideograms, enabling the activation of vibranium energy (V. Johnson 2018).

Scholars have looked at embodied knowledges—be they cognitive, physical, or a combination—as a way to better understand how practitioners improvise to make things and apply knowledge using new concepts. TVC improvisation is a shared practice among practitioners who draw on embodied experiences that can be translated into geographic or spatial coordinates, music compositions, visual designs, language systems, and digital and physical artifacts. Though the practitioners have different intentions when using improvisation, they all make spontaneous choices, often without recourse to a set plan.

Improvisational Storytelling and Fabrication

Computational theorists explore the temporal qualities of making and the rules that structure and take apart what is being made (Knight 2015). One such arrangement is the score, a notation system that contains single or multiple parts in a composition. Sherri Lynn Wood (2015) compares the jazz score to quilt making as an improvisational performance. Improvisational quilts connect with embodied representations that capture direct physical experiences that are intertwined with the movement of the body. Call-and-response participation and similar methods can be linked to Wood's term "showing up," which describes the performance aspects of improvisational quilting (Wood 2015, 105). These methods are used to establish meaningful connections among seemingly disparate elements.

The vehicle for learning how to improvise is the score, which, like the lead sheet in jazz composition, captures essential elements and provides basic steps and arrangements while leaving room for interpretation and variation. The scoring process includes rules and a set of notations or parameters within which the improvisation is free to take shape (Wood 2015, 106), like the A-B-A-B-A rhythm pattern in "Cold Sweat" mentioned in chapter 3 and the groove that is produced when playing the pattern. Instead of musical notes, the score for an improvisational quilt generates a glossary of shapes that a quilt maker can improvise with.

"Showing up" in music or quilt composing involves continuous performing and prototyping. Improvisational quilts show dissimilar, sometimes evolving elements—often juxtaposed in a single piece (Leon 1998). This is similar to nonlinear storytelling that presents events in ways that do not follow linear patterns. The disruptive characteristic of these processes forms a basis for improvisation that can be seen in Gee's Bend quilting in Alabama. Gee's Bend quilts have a visual relationship with textiles from West and Central Africa (see Wahlman 2001) that are part of a common *design vernacular* (see Mack 2012) and a generative grammar.

Generative grammars formalize heritage algorithms, which, as we have seen, have underused computational potential in cultural arts (Bennett 2016). The heritage algorithms in African textiles were studied by the Generative Design Team from Concordia University. The team applied a generative model to interpret the geometric structure inherent in Kuba textiles by ascribing a shape grammar to create contemporary design variations through grammar variations and to fabricate the new designs on a computerized loom (Rajagopalan et al. 2006). This research shows how using simple variations could generate, in their corresponding grammars, interesting families of artworks.

The generative and making grammars of TVC practices and activities are enacted and interpreted by makers who are skilled in a particular craft . The process of making in Kuba textiles and Gee's Bend quilts is a kind of performance, and naming the rules becomes a kind of game (Wood 2015; Mack 2012). Sherri Lynn Wood's "rhythmic grid" score framework describes Marzella Tatum's quilt making, which uses variation by arranging blocks in a way that makes sense to her (Leon 1998). These craft performances incorporate spontaneity and improvisation in designs to achieve uniqueness and individuality, part of the maker's aesthetics or style, which is most often achieved by the juxtaposition of distinct geometric motifs and by controlled variations in visual and rhythmic elements.

Tangible Improvisation with Mnemonic Devices

Mnemonic devices are memory aids, and they play an important role in improvisation. These devices organize and encode information to make things more memorable (Roberts and Roberts 1996). Algorithmic designs and performances that are created from memory and through improvisation can be transmitted with devices that enable human interaction, which includes the embodiment of data, whole-body interaction, and the embedding of tangible (touch-based) interfaces in different spaces and contexts. Tangible user interfaces such as the multitouch digital lukasa table described in chapter 4 help users collaborate better, create personal stories from a lexicon of artifacts, and perceive computational problem-solving as more engaging or playful.

Heritage artifacts such as the cosmogram and its various representations draw from methods of *iterative design* that allow artists and craftspeople to come up with prototypes, or new and different ways to make things. Iterative design is improvisational and applies doing and sensing (see Knight and Stiny 2015, 12) to craft performances—taking parts of a project and then using what has been created to inform and serve as a starting point for adding additional elements. This process elicits call-and-response participation of multiple users—*speakers* whose role is to sense and respond to the environment and *listeners* who, in turns, translate the speaker's actions and often change roles to become a speaker. The performance is an algorithm.

Mnemonic devices such as the ring shout (Kongo Cosmogram), Native American powwow circle, John Coltrane's "Giant Steps" design, or the rhythmic chorus in "Cold Sweat" are amenable to algorithmic design, or rules, for patterns of repetition and improvisation. Wood's "rhythmic grid" score for quilts is another example of an improvisational framework. Artists build on these cultural frameworks, and teachers can use their artwork as scaffolds to STEAM learning. Students can embody these artifacts and performances while learning how to translate vernacular knowledge into geometry (Eglash 2004), computer science (Eglash et al. 2006), or into algebraic thinking with ratios, fractions, and polyrhythms (Sharp and Stevens 2007).

What is important to take away from this chapter is that TVC improvisation can support culturally relevant making and help students apply STEAM concepts to the making process. Students can learn to situate this cultural production in academic subjects. They learn how making in these contexts connects to familiar activities: break dancing, music production, visual art, crafts, and the like. This type of learning makes STEAM more meaningful and involves students' histories, identities, and emotions.

6

Improvisational STEAM Learning and Making

Inspired by the embodied interaction in hip-hop cyphers, graffiti tagging, and Indigenous electronic music powwows, the "Electrofunk Mixtape" explored the connections between computational action, making, improvisation through live performance, and STEAM learning in Taos, New Mexico. Elder Marie Reyna, director of the Oo-Oo-Nah Art Center at the Taos Pueblo, helped recruit ten elementary and middle school–age Indigenous (Tiwa) youth to work with six Taos High School students and visiting teaching artists as part of a three-day workshop sponsored by STEMarts, an educational nonprofit. Participants riffed on the mixtape—a compilation of songs—and combined electronics with interactive, outdoor performances. STEAM activities culminated in sculptural installations, outdoor projections, and live performances at the Paseo Project festival in Taos.

STEMarts workshop participants improvised with different electronic elements for live events in and around Taos. They explored artwork such as "Pull of the Moon" by Bert Benally and Ai Weiwei and experienced A Tribe Called Red's "Stadium Pow Wow" as a music visualization. Participants learned how to make wearable and sculptural objects embedded with sensors that detected sound waves and converted the sound waves to colors. They learned how to solder electronic components and used circuit breadboards to insert light-emitting diodes (LEDs) into the sculptures. On the final day of the workshop, participants learned how to use software to map sound-generated animations onto buildings and assembled everything for the live outdoor performances.

TVC improvisation links STEAM learning to *thinking tools* such as imaging and visualizing and to thinking kinesthetically, transforming data into visual forms, and understanding data and experiments both kinesthetically and empathetically (Root-Bernstein and Root-Bernstein 2013). These tools are often taught in arts and crafts classes, which are in decline in public education because K–12 curricula in many US schools focus primarily on STEM and verbal skills. Arts and crafts develop habits of thought and action such as problem-solving and provide new structures, methods, and analogies that can stimulate innovation. This chapter shows how TVC improvisation can help educators rethink the links among performance, STEAM learning, and culturally relevant maker habits of mind.

This chapter looks at how improvisation helps learners undertake complex ideas and tasks on the fly. TVC improvisation is a *meaning-making* activity by which people interpret and respond to situations, events, artifacts, or prompts, in the light of their prior knowledge and experiences (Zittoun and Brinkmann 2012). These experiences enable them to act, think, and feel in ways that are important to themselves and their communities. The STEMarts workshop merged TVC improvisation with *cultural modeling* (see Lee 2001) to scaffold the participants' existing knowledge and support their acquisition of technology skills. After being recruited by Pueblo elders, Indigenous youth went to the Taos high school makerspace, bringing with them their own cultural capital. The makerspace was where the youth practiced being makers, and the experience increased their *STEAM* knowledge, attitudes, experiences, and resources.

For three days STEMarts participants explored embodied knowledge and ethnocomputational creativity (see Bennett 2016) as a way to focus on TVC. Take, for example, call-and-response participation—a rhetorical performance (see Smitherman 2000, 150) that includes improvisational language, cultural relevance and values, and involvement with and immersion in events and situations. In line with this tradition, STEMarts youth took part in live performances that were facilitated by the use of call-and-response. Participants learned how to use electronic and digital technology—wearable devices, mobile apps, music visuals, and projection mapping—in ways that created sensory and physical experiences for the participants and their audiences, helping them acquire new tools and habits.

The STEMarts workshop merged physical computing with art and culture to explore how TVC improvisation can connect youths' lived experiences with making and to help them take on more complex tasks. Workshop activities drew on *models of competence* (see Nasir et al. 2005) such as participants' knowledge of hip-hop, electronic dance music, and Taos Puebloan (Tiwa) artifacts. This approach is supported by research that positions making with tools that align, theoretically, with embodiment and improvisation (Hagerman and Cotnam-Kappel 2019). The workshop comprised three phases: hands-on interaction with artifacts and materials, the use of sensors that respond to the environment, and the use of technology with rhetorical performances to interact with the Taos community at outdoor live events.

Learning and Building Community through TVC Improvisation

STEMarts used the *forming, storming, norming, performing* model of group development (see Tuckman 1965) to create every element of the workshop, including the "Electrofunk Mixtape" live performances. The workshop brought two groups together: the middle school–age Taos Pueblo youth and Taos High School students. Participants were first oriented to project tasks and then to one another. They explored examples of culturally relevant and environmentally responsive outdoor art such as "Pull of the Moon" by Bert Benally and Ai Weiwei and videos by A Tribe Called Red. They assisted in preparing for the live, interactive outdoor performances that consisted of physical and digital artifacts that produce sounds, lights, and other effects.

During the storming and norming phases, participants sorted themselves out according to their personal interests and gained each other's trust. This was the "doing and sensing to make stuff" (see Knight and Stiny 2015, 12) part of the workshop. Participants explored technological doodling and thinkering using Adafruit's PianoGlove, which senses and "plays" colors visually and aurally, and Figure, a mobile app based on the Roland TR-808 drum machine, to compose electrofunk music, which combines electronic music and hip-hop. Electronic sound sensors were added to circuit breadboards as a base for prototyping sculptures that lit up and responded to music played by a DJ (figure 6.1). Participants learned how to solder electronic components and programmed wearable microcontrollers to make their own versions of the PianoGlove.

For the final, performing phase, workshop participants assembled their multimedia mixtape by assembling outdoors the stuff they made in the high school makerspace. The "Electrofunk Mixtape" was the live performance part of the STEMarts experience that gave Taos youth and their communities an opportunity to experience what they created. STEMarts participants learned how to be VJs—live performers of visuals at public events—and used modular music visualization software to manipulate media such as effects and live video (figure 6.2). STEMarts invited the Taos community to participate in the creation of the sound-generated imagery, and software was used to project and map the video on outdoor walls.

Figure 6.1
The STEMarts workshop in Taos, New Mexico, quickly engaged Indigenous youth with the creation and use of electronic devices.
Photo: Nettrice Gaskins. Courtesy of STEMarts.

The STEMarts workshop and live events drew on the capacity of young people to move and act in their communities, to use their senses and bodies to explore the properties of different materials, and to perform new actions for increasingly challenging purposes with a range of technologies (Abrahamson and Lindgren 2014). Workshop participants took inspiration from *electronic powwows*, also referred to as *virtual sounding spaces*, which build community through the shared space of the dance floor (Woloshyn 2015; Weheliye 2005). Alexa Woloshyn notes that performers and audiences at A Tribe Called Red's electronic powwows "listen through the body as the powwow resonates" (2015, 2). "Electrofunk Mixtape" events created similar kinesthetic listening experiences in Taos when the STEMarts VJs collaborated with the local DJ Oliver Knight.

Figure 6.2
The Taos Pueblo youth playing the role of VJs at the "Electrofunk Mixtape" perfor-
mance in Taos, New Mexico.
Photo: Nettrice Gaskins. Courtesy of STEMarts.

Two years later, elements of the STEMarts workshop in Taos were
adapted for use with sixteen high school students in the Advanced
Placement (AP) Computer Science Principles (CSP) course at Boston
Arts Academy. The College Board's AP CSP curriculum framework
was scaffolded with culturally relevant making, embodied knowledge, and ethnocomputational creativity. The students met in the
school's STEAM Lab to learn how to use coding to generate heritage
algorithms and translate them into physical objects. For example,
students learned how to use the Processing programming platform
to generate designs that were laser etched into materials and put on
display in the school's gallery. The students also participated in a
three-day workshop with the Rensselaer Polytechnic Institute professor Audrey Bennett.

For the first part of Bennett's workshop, the AP CSP students were divided into smaller groups to research quilt making, learn about quilting practices, and present their findings. Their options included quilts from Appalachia; Gee's Bend, Alabama; and the Lakota and Anishinaabe tribes. Next, the students used culturally situated design tools to simulate their chosen quilt patterns (figure 6.3). As a last step, Bennett showed the students how to physically engage with their CSDT designs by improvising with fabric and materials to produce patchwork quilts. Later, the AP CSP students, along with the STEAM Lab, hosted a pop-up event in Boston Arts Academy's cafeteria as part of Hour of Code to celebrate computer science. Other students performed along with the sound-generated imagery created by the AP CSP students.

The AP CSP students worked with the school's theater department to produce a staged performance of *The Wiz*, adapted from L. Frank Baum's *The Wonderful Wizard of Oz* novel. The character Herman Smith/the Wiz was performed off stage; the actor's lines were recorded and imported into the music visualization software to create different scenes. As a result, the actor's voice appeared on stage as music visuals that were projected and mapped to the ceiling. The effect gave the Wiz character an otherworldly, omnipresent appearance in the space (figure 6.4). Also, on display in the theater lobby were elements of the workshop with Bennett that included printouts of the students' computer-generated designs and their physical quilts with electronics—microcontrollers and LEDs—embedded in them.

The takeaways from STEMarts in Taos and the STEAM Lab in Boston is that TVC improvisation can create meaningful STEAM experiences and build kinship among students in a constructionist sense (Przybylla and Romeike 2014; Papert 1980). Merging culture, coding, and electronics to make things interactive emphasizes the importance of physicality in STEAM learning and motivates underrepresented ethnic students to use new applications. In the classroom or lab, or on a stage, TVC improvisation invites the use of

Figure 6.3
Students work with Audrey Bennett to create physical quilts in the STEAM Lab at Boston Arts Academy.
Photo: Nettrice Gaskins. Courtesy of Boston Arts Academy.

cultural artifacts, maker materials, and digital tools to create immersive experiences. It develops students' sense of agency and supports the learning of multiple literacies, critical and creative problem-solving, and collaboration skills. Cultural and community events such as live pop-up events and theatrical performances can be sites for high engagement in STEAM.

"Sounding Smart," Embodied Creativity, and the Stage

Three dance students entered the STEAM Lab at Boston Arts Academy with an idea for an extra-credit chemistry project. They brought with them knowledge they had gained of themselves and the practice of

Figure 6.4
Boston Arts Academy's theatrical production of *The Wiz* included sound-generated, quilt-based animations projected above the stage at the Strand Theater in Boston, Massachusetts.
Photo: Nettrice Gaskins.

dance. Unlike the STEMarts youth in Taos, these students had regular access to maker materials such as Electric Paint, a viscous, carbon-based substance that replaces electrical wire in physical computing projects, and Touch Boards with touch sensors to make projects interactive. The students came up with an idea for an interactive dance floor as a MIDI controller. They found a tutorial on a website and learned about how artists use conductive materials and electronics to make art interactive (Bare Conductive 2020).

In addition to making an electronic dance floor, the students looked up the material properties of conductive paint and how it interacted with Touch Boards to create sounds. To motivate the students, teachers, and lab staff adopted an *inquiry-based learning* method (see Bayram et al. 2013) that poses questions such as "How does the paint conduct energy?" and "What is carbon (graphite) and how is it conductive?" To describe the molecular structure of graphite, used to make the paint, one student read, "Hexagons are linked together on a flat plane that allows what?" Another student responded as the other wrote, "Electrons to move from atom to atom." After doing their research, the students applied their science knowledge to the dance floor project.

As they worked on their project, the students became more self-assured about their ability to acquire and use science knowledge in physical computing. They demonstrated multiple cognitive processes such as recording what they discovered (using a laptop and pen and paper) and recording what they said (using a mobile app on a smartphone). After talking about what she had learned, one student said, "Oh, yes. That sounds smart!" because she had suddenly realized that she had gained a firmer grasp of the subject. Once the students could explain how the paint was made, they had to choreograph a dance for an end-of-semester school performance. Here, sounding smart correlates to understanding or sensemaking, which is a situated activity.

The students' circuit design consisted of a series of shapes and lines that roughly copied the molecular structure of carbon. At the high school's end-of-semester student showcase, the "smarter" dance students installed their electronic dance floor, and one student performed barefoot on the floor by stepping on different parts of the Electric Paint circuit to trigger different sounds (figure 6.5). The Touch Board for the dance floor was connected to a laptop with digital audio software installed on it. During the student's dance performance, she demonstrated embodied improvisation by moving as a carbon electron moves from atom to atom. She was fully engaged in spontaneously creating these movements, which were facilitated through dance and a creative exploration of technology.

The chemistry-dance project at the academy is an example of doodling with technology and "geeking out" that demonstrates

Figure 6.5
A Boston Arts Academy dance student performs on her group's painted circuit to demonstrate electroconductivity at Boston Arts Academy.
Photo: Nettrice Gaskins. Courtesy of Boston Arts Academy.

intense student commitment with technology (Itō, Baumer, and Bittanti 2019). The process of making through TVC improvisation equipped students with new sensory motor skills, laying a foundation for an embodied understanding of themselves as agents in the world with their own interests and experiences. TVC improvisation advances theories such as *learning by doing* (see Dewey 1897 [1940]), *learning by making* (see Martinez and Stager 2019), and *learning by sensemaking* (see Knight 2015) to emphasize students' cultural and personal ways of being, knowing, and doing.

In addition to using touch-based devices to sense and interact with things, students can use devices that require no hand contact or touching. At Boston Arts Academy, visual-arts students practiced gesture drawing while experimenting with the Leap motion

Figure 6.6
Visual-arts students experiment with gesture drawing using Leap motion controllers in the STEAM Lab at Boston Arts Academy.
Photo: Nettrice Gaskins.

controller (figure 6.6). Leap controllers are small sensors that are analogous to a computer mouse. Students learned how to program Leap devices using Processing, a language that was built to teach visual artists and designers the fundamentals of computer programming. By changing values and variables in the code, the students changed the way digital objects are drawn (e.g., color and line thickness). While demonstrating how data is transformed into images, this activity can also encourage students to learn coding.

Performing with electronic and interactive devices can help students gradually develop new perceptual-motor schemas that allow them to use tools in increasingly sophisticated and novel ways and to develop functional metaphors (e.g., the dance floor–carbon interface) for higher-order concepts (Hagerman and Cotnam-Kappel

2019). In-the-moment feedback in response to students' questions and hands-on coaching move students toward deeper expertise. When students are immersed in and performing with technology, as opposed to passively viewing it on a screen, they can more easily make the transition from hanging out and messing around to geeking out (see Itō, Baumer, and Bittanti 2019) with technology.

Building Blocks of Improvisational Learning

Improvisation has a positive impact on cognitive processes such as divergent thinking, flexibility, language, memory, problem-solving, co-construction, and everyday life experiences (Lubart 2001). TVC improvisation involves *modularity*, or the degree to which system components or modules can be used in embodied interaction and sensemaking. Sounds, visual motifs, blocks of code, or the y-shaped plaits that make up a cornrow braid are basic building blocks for improvisation. Modules can be repeated, transformed, or manipulated in different ways. The term also refers to the process of constructing a project comprising a collection of components that carry out specified functions, such as generating algorithmic designs and creating "interactive intelligences" or AI (see Thórisson et al. 2004) using code blocks, physical devices, and tangible and virtual interfaces.

Modular tools such as block-based visual programming (software) can engage embodied interactions that address the agentive action of mind (what is learned from the activity), brain (what is learned from adaptation), and body (what is learned from experience). For example, STEMarts participants and Boston Arts Academy students learned how to use modular tools to manipulate different types of media such as 3D models, quilt designs, live videos, and photos. They became proficient at *mindful copying*, which relied on their observations and choices on what and how to copy (El-Zanfaly 2015, 90). In addition to this, live performances involved students in the cyclic process of iteration as they learned to improvise with artifacts and tools.

STEMarts and BAA students were given access to a variety of tools with which they made things and engaged others. Music visualization (VJ) software allowed them to create a map of connected modules to control shape (polygon), translation, scaling, iteration of parts of a scene, and so on. Students learned how to listen to and feel what the DJ was playing, then adjusted different parameters to create visuals that corresponded with the music. Students also invited their communities to assist them in the creation of sound-generated imagery using a live video module (figure 6.7). The students' embodied interaction with modular tools and artifacts compares to the way break-dancers respond to music in a freestyle cypher or the communal experience of kinesthetic listening at an electronic powwow.

TVC improvisation also uses a collection, or *patchwork*, of educational methods, allowing teachers to move from a deficit model to one that builds on students' tacit knowledge and understanding through questioning and facilitation. This model includes inquiry, community building, and the use of aesthetic tools of cultural relevance to deploy whatever strategies, methods, or empirical materials that are at hand. This *improvisational patchwork* approach to STEAM teaching is inspired by the framework of Sherri Lynn Wood (2015) who annotated the improvisational design work of quilters into scores that correspond loosely to musical notation and storytelling. *Improvisational patchwork learning* makes use of self-contained chunks of instruction and invites teachers to be like VJs by responding to challenges in the environment and inserting culturally relevant modules into their existing curricular frameworks and plans.

In this learning scenario, students can offer feedback that enables teachers to prototype and test new ideas, make improvements, identify potential problems, and ultimately determine whether an activity or project is engaging and meets the learning objectives.

Figure 6.7
Taos Pueblo youth demonstrate their VJ skill with Magic Music Visuals at the Luna Chapel pop-up event in Taos.
Photo: Nettrice Gaskins. Courtesy of STEMarts.

Reframing the roles of the teacher-designer and student-playtester who cocreate learning experiences establishes a new perspective on the relationship between embodied improvisation, STEAM learning, and technological agency. For example, the use of the design cypher in a hip-hop architecture camp brought together practitioners and students who created designs in a fast-paced, cross-disciplinary environment (Runcie 2018). The cypher culminated in the creation of a virtual reality project.

This learning process was explored during the development of an educational game as a way to reinforce understanding of key science concepts and help students acquire spatial reasoning and decision-making skills. *Home: The Bacteria Project* was developed as part of a multi-year initiative that brought together professional artists, high school art teachers, and scientists to find ways to make exploring the human microbiome more engaging for students. The goal of the project was to reframe the human body ecologically as colonies of creatures and transform notions of human health, predisposition to disease, and treatment and medication. What makes *Home* unique is that it made use of heritage artifacts such as the cosmogram.

Lead teachers for the initiative worked with scientists to identify core science concepts that would need to be translated into game-play. Then a team was assembled to make connections between the story content and the game's design. The game repurposes the Kongo Cosmogram—a map of the universe through the lens of Kongo culture—to provide alternative meanings to the scientific concepts. Game components were modeled on visual elements and cultural concepts such as *kalunga*, the watery boundary between the world of the living and the world of the dead in Congo religions. The game's story traces the journey of the main character (from life to death and back) using *kalunga*.

The art teachers created the concept art and 3D characters for the game and students were recruited to playtest and help develop the game levels. By playing the game, students learn about what happens in the body when someone eats spoiled food. Players enter a sick girl's body through her mouth to become immersed in the story's events and interact with different heritage artifacts. To win the game, students must find their way down the throat where they find a full representation of the Kongo Cosmogram. They must release water (kalunga) to open a portal to the stomach where the girl can be healed (figure 6.8). There, players encounter microbes that colonize the human body; they also learn what happens when the body recovers.

From dancing to embody the movement of carbon molecules to using touch-based devices and interfaces for sensing things, to game playtesting to learn about the inner workings of the human body, the use of technology to explore new concepts has shown

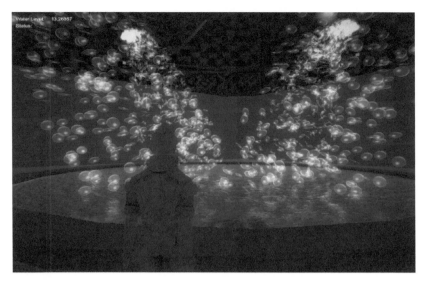

Figure 6.8
What players see when they reach the kalunga portal to the stomach in *Home: The Bacteria Project*.
Photo: Nettrice Gaskins. Courtesy of John Adekoje.

promise as strategies to engage learners, especially students from ethnic groups underrepresented in STEAM. Embodied interaction connects learning to physical action through creative prototyping and the manipulation of modules. Activities that involve improvisation have been shown to increase participants' degree of perceived self-efficacy, self-reported creative feeling, and cognitive flow. TVC improvisation contributes to this work by demonstrating how cultural practices (and artifacts created from these practices) can enhance making and STEAM learning.

IV   TVC and Culturally Relevant Making

7

TVC and Implications for STEAM Teaching and Learning

Equity has been a serious problem facing maker and STEAM education programs, specifically along the lines of *access* (who has the keys?), *diversity* (who is in the room?), and *inclusion* (who feels welcome?). Research shows that underrepresented ethnic groups have unique learning and meaning-making experiences that differ from mainstream groups (Scott, Sheridan, and Clark 2014). As demonstrated previously, these groups use technology in ways that are linked to their histories, legacies, and social locations (Nelson and Tu 2001). Additionally, studies show that, whereas enrollment of underrepresented ethnic groups in postsecondary schools is increasing (de Brey et al. 2019), advancement of these groups in STEM fields continues to decrease (NSF/NCSES 2017).

Underrepresented ethnic groups are vulnerable to societal influences that inevitably assert dominant cultural values and norms (Vossoughi, Hooper, and Escudé 2016). The TVC framework makes a case for emphasizing the importance of understanding multiethnic, multilingual, and multidisciplinary characteristics of culturally diverse communities as they relate to both cultural art (generally) and STEAM learning. Including these cultural practices in the maker movement and in maker education requires being intentional in creating space so practitioners from those groups feel a sense of belonging and feel that their work is valued (Gomes 2016). This space must include acknowledgement that underrepresented ethnic groups may experience, express, or see things differently from other groups and that these experiences, expressions, and perceptions are recognized and valued.

Cultural practices such as reusing found materials and performing through craft making overlap with the everyday lived experiences of students and the power of *learning by doing* (Martinez and Stager 2019). These activities and settings stand in stark contrast to the existing works, practices, and environments of nondominant ethnic practitioners. Current understandings of how people develop expertise indicate that school learning is deficient in distributing adaptive expertise across groups and in promoting the sociocultural significance of content. This book addresses these issues by expanding the definition of technology and maker practice and by connecting technical literacy, diversity, and culture through the frame of the *techno-vernacular*, which centers creative innovations produced by overlooked ethnic communities.

Underrepresented ethnic practitioners are actively engaged in making, and they persist despite the effects of exclusion and nonengagement. This book theorizes that these TVC modes of activity should be accessible for all students in order to engage those who otherwise would not voluntarily participate in STEAM and conventional making. Action is needed from researchers and educators to create culturally relevant and inclusive experiences for underrepresented ethnic students in schools and out-of-school-time programs.

This book offers a range of solutions and examples that can support the inclusion and engagement of underrepresented ethnic groups—adopting TVC reappropriation to foster the reclamation of artifacts from dominant culture (for creative and learning purposes), leveraging remixing that encourages tinkering with things, and encouraging improvisation that involves the spontaneous and inventive use of materials. Through TVC, STEAM learning can be couched in socially significant learning contexts such as live and interactive performances. Cultural artifacts used by TVC practitioners are often amenable to computational methods and electronic (embodied) interactions. The primary difference between the TVC examples and more mainstream making projects sits at the level of cultural practice, more specifically with the tacit knowledge, deeper assumptions, and habits that influence the ways people create things.

Key ideas that amplify TVC remixing in labs or classrooms include design mapping that makes use of cultural artifacts that are algorithmic and grammars that enable doing and seeing with shapes (Knight and Stiny 2015). TVC reappropriation builds on the mapping concept to introduce new concepts such as modular prototyping with things that can be readily repurposed and doodling (see Dixon 2015) with digital tools and found materials to solve problems and broaden the maker mind-set among students. TVC draws on the cultural knowledge of improvisation to build on computational making theories that involve seeing, sensemaking, iteration, embodied interaction, and rhetorical performance.

Although many of the examples mentioned in the book are not considered to be STEAM, they deeply explore integrated STEAM concepts and can give educators another way to approach STEAM learning. Recent research found that when teachers think about personalized learning, very few of them consider cultural relevance (Leshnick, Allen, and Berman 2019). It is more common for teachers to think about students' learning preferences or career interests than their cultural backgrounds. Teaching culturally relevant making and STEAM activities is very important because it empowers students to learn to express themselves and function in a more diverse world. Educators are in need of more concrete examples to be able to customize education that meets their students' personal interests and cultural knowledge and that, in turn, can connect their schoolwork to activities outside formal classrooms.

Looking Outward, Inward, and Forward

Culturally relevant pedagogy and instructional materials can play important roles in helping systematically remove prejudices about race and class and in honoring students' diverse backgrounds (Chiefs for Change 2019). The recognition and inclusion of DIY maker practices in ethnic communities reflect the diversity of America's students. Scholars suggest starting with the assumption that practices resonant with making already exist in diverse forms in all communities. Lisa Schwartz and Kris Gutiérrez state that "inventing, making, tinkering, designing are indigenous practices, that is, practices that originate and occur naturally in particular ecologies" (2015, 577).

Rather than working to take making to nondominant communities, this assumption of human ingenuity (McDermott and Raley 2011) positions practitioners as learners, too, inquiring into the ways of asking, knowing, and relating involved in existing forms of making (Vossoughi, Hooper, and Escudé 2016). The ways that making and equity are conceptualized can either restrict or expand the possibility that the growing maker movement will contribute to "intellectually generative and liberatory educational experiences for . . . students of color" (211). TVC and similar frameworks can help researchers and educators envision an equitable, culturally relevant maker-learning program, including *looking outward* to the local community to find examples of practices that involve designing, tinkering, or fixing things; *looking inward* to examine areas where making habits of mind and learning may already exist; and *looking forward* to help learners cultivate agency and feel a sense of ownership and belonging.

One example of this multipronged approach is the OX4D Plays project. The project was a collaboration with Community Design Resource Center director Susan Rogers, the artist Carrie Schneider, Avenue Community Development Corporation, the Houston Housing Authority, University of Houston AIAS Freedom by Design, five teen interns from Oxford Place Apartments, and residents. For looking outward, the design team brought in neighborhood photos on which residents could draw or write (Lewis 2017). Residents were given the prompt "What would inspire you to play here?" Their feedback led to the design team's plan that included Play Courts, Play Spots, and Play Zones, the latter of which included designated sidewalks and paths for active play.

One of the Play Courts is a tangible, modular design (see modularity in chapter 6) that allows interactions between residents and a stage that unfolds in three dimensions. As part of the design process, the project team explored Afrofuturism and repurposed the cosmogram with youth who designed circular motifs that were painted on the stage (figure 7.1). A freestyle rap performance at the staged Play Court conveyed the meaning of looking forward, by making the built 3D space into a site of live performance. Carrie Schneider told me via email that the timing of the project overlapped with the police shooting of a local resident. She says,

> We sat down with the teens and said "Look, I know it's absurd to think about play right now. It is actually less absurd to imagine having space in outer space and in future time than to imagine play right here right now." So we introduced them to Afrofuturism. (March 2, 2017)

The OX4D Plays design team engaged residents and drew from them their knowledge and experiences to create replicable, scalable installations in neighborhoods. Afrofuturism, which is mentioned

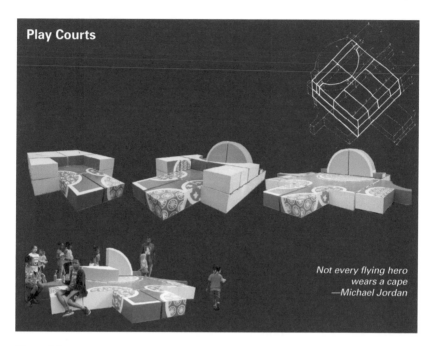

Play Courts

*Not every flying hero
wears a cape
—Michael Jordan*

Figure 7.1
OX4D Play Court portable stage.
Photo: Susan Rogers. Courtesy of Community Design Resource Center, University of Houston, Susan Rogers, Barbara Blanco, Adelle Main, Tran Le; artist Carrie Schneider; youth interns Canard Smith, Trayvin Walton, Tre'veon Hunt, Franchesca Addison, Porschea Davis; HTX Made, Stage Fabrication.

several times in this book, is in the domain of the speculative—addressing present issues by honoring the past and looking forward. Afrofuturism provides an intersectional lens through which practitioners can view possible futures or alternate realities. Artists such as Ayodamola Okunseinde of *Iyapo Repository* use speculative design to connect cultural artifacts and performances to bring social justice issues to light, for open discussion. The young people involved in OX4D Plays were encouraged to do the same.

Projects like OX4D Plays have implications for integrating culturally relevant making and distributed learning in STEAM-related curriculum design through the adaptation and reinterpretation of cultural artifacts, physical environments, and virtual environments using concepts such as biomechanical cyborgs, electronic dance performances, multimedia mixtape production, and interactive "playable" mural making. These works leverage cultural practices and student experiences as creative modes for new and alternative STEAM learning methods and platforms.

Getting Down and Showing Up

The term "getting down" refers to a common practice in hip-hop of sampling sections of songs called breaks, then using those breaks to intensify audience anticipation, signal the start of something new, or create variety in the arrangements. "Showing up" involves the continuous process of performing and prototyping, similar to what happens during improvisational quilt making (Wood 2015). Artists who use these practices bring with them a wealth of cultural knowledge, including how their work connects to STEAM topics. With this in mind, a research project sponsored by the National Science Foundation (NSF 2013) sought to (1) engage dialogue among notable STEM experts and artists, (2) advance understanding of the potential impacts of culturally relevant making, arts-based learning, and research that can extend participation and understanding of STEM, and (3) build capacity for sustained collaboration for the benefit of research and practice.

The research project culminated in a transdisciplinary workshop, Advancing STEM through Culturally Situated Arts-Based Learning, that included keynote presentations, design mapping, and synergistic activities for participants and the community. Among the activities was a creative social featuring a live performance by Sanford Biggers and his multimedia concept band Moon Medicin, which performs against a backdrop of digital artifacts. Participating artists were Biggers and Vanessa Ramos-Velasquez (who were the keynote speakers), Xenobia Bailey, Destiny Palmer, John Jennings, Will Wilson, Audrey Bennett, Michi Meko, L'Merchie Frazier, and James Eugene. The STEM experts were Celia Pearce, Jacqueline Royster, Anita McKeown, Jamila Cola, Ron Eglash, Laura Lieberman, Roger Malina, Harvey Seifter, Donna Whiting, and Lynn Goldsmith.

The participating artists were chosen because their artworks serve as cultural models for STEM learning in ways that are context bound—tied to the everyday practices of diverse groups and constructed using local and indigenous knowledge. The STEM experts sought a clearer understanding of how their art and TVC practices connect to STEM subjects. During the design mapping session, the deeper meanings embedded in the artists' works were decoded and a common language was sought with STEM experts to support meaningful dialogue across subject areas and disciplines. Participants were asked, "How do culturally situated design tools and strategies engage students from underrepresented ethnic groups?" The mapping exercise uncovered broad themes that connected to the artists' works (figure 7.2).

Evaluators from the Findings Group used Social Network Analysis to assess the role that the workshop played in not only influencing individuals but also encouraging potential collaboration. Through quantitative analysis they identified the connections that participants made across bodies of knowledge, found that those connections formed potential for future collaborations, and showed that the participants had achieved their main goal (collaboration) for attending the workshop. In a survey performed after the workshop, participants recommended building spaces where TVC practices, art, and STEM subjects could be explored.

Riffing and Putting Ideas into Action

To "riff" means to improvise on a subject by extending a singular idea or inspiration into a practice or habit. In jazz, blues, and other

Figure 7.2
Advancing STEM through Culturally Situated Arts-Based Learning workshop partici-
pants in a design mapping activity at Georgia Tech.
Photo: Nettrice Gaskins.

musical genres, riffs are short rhythmic, melodic, or harmonic figures that are repeated to establish the framework of a song. Riffs are
often paired with call-and-response to create cyclical patterns or iterations. This book riffs on making by expanding the breadth, depth,
and scope of STEAM education. Projects highlighted in the book
apply TVC modes of activity to computational action and thinking
tools (see Root-Bernstein 2001) such as visualization, pattern recognition, body thinking, empathizing, dimensional thinking, modeling, and playing. These tools are in greater need in STEAM labs and
classrooms yet are not taught in many public schools.

Future-facing schools and educational programs must teach culturally relevant making and tinkering skills to all students and include
computational action and design in the core curriculum. Approaches

include reconceptualizing maker culture and enhancing mainstream maker activities with the creative innovations produced in underrepresented ethnic communities. TVC shows how nondominant practices merge Indigenous and outside knowledge. These modes open pathways into making and STEAM that support recognizing, and learning from, ethnic communities of practice. At the same time, TVC challenges the labeling of specific populations as interest deficient rather than becoming familiar with the communities and seeking to understand their subjective experiences and critiques (Nasir and Vakil 2017).

The intellectual depth of everyday cultural practices and how these practices connect to academic subjects in meaningful ways is of interest to many scholars who study ways to support the repurposing of mainstream approaches to making toward new ends. This research can inform the selection of materials, tools, and activities and the ways teachers talk about making and STEAM. Examples featured in this book address informal and formal learning experiences that confront normative understandings of STEAM ingenuity, particularly with regard to *who* we see as inventors, *what* we see as creativity, and *on whose terms* their ideas and practices are valued (Vossoughi, Hooper, and Escudé 2016).

Research by Dina El-Zanfaly (2015) shows that sensory experiences—the direct and iterative engagement with materials, tools, machines, and things—reinforce the maker's ability to create. We see this in hip-hop when practitioners repurpose discarded devices and adapt technology to suit their needs. Grandmaster Flash's use of electronics to isolate breakbeats can show students how to break down complex real-world issues into more manageable parts. Teachers can also apply this example to engineering design and connecting everyday materials to computational devices. Culturally relevant making can reinforce in students the value of imitation, iteration, and improvisation (see El-Zanfaly 2015) through the use of visual coding and use of touch- and motion-based sensing devices that are the next digital frontier for K–12 STEAM education.

Making things that replicate and sustain cultural practices such as TVC can, as noted by Sylvia Martinez (2015) open doors and blur the lines between teachers and learners. To begin to cultivate these learning opportunities, teachers and students must have time, space, and access to physical and digital tools and materials. This includes access to digital tools like Makey Makey electronic boards and Touch Board MIDI interfaces, especially to create physical prototypes that inspire the ideation and design process. Learning through culturally relevant making and TVC modes merges the maker habits with computational action through the application of, for example, culturally situated design tools (Lachney 2017) and making things that foster collaboration, communication, and meaning making through physically shared objects in the real world.

By exploring various strategies, students can choose methods that are "personal and insightful" to help move them toward becoming more flexible and adaptive (Mercier and Higgins 2013). Elementary school students can learn about cultural designs and the geometric attributes of polygons, symmetry, transformations, patterns and shapes, similarity, ratios, and functional models of geometric figures. Chapter 2 looks at middle school students who learned how 2D cultural designs were congruent to others if the second ones were obtained from the first by a sequence of rotations, reflections, and translations using physical and digital tools. High school students can build on their understanding of congruence in cultural designs by exploring similarity and symmetry, which can be understood from the perspective of geometric transformation.

Other avenues for STEAM exploration include biomimicry, which imitates natural models, systems, and elements to solve problems; biomechanics, which looks at the structure, function, and motion of mechanical aspects of biological systems; and kinetics, which studies the energy generated by moving objects. Teachers can use media to make concepts culturally relevant, increase motivation, and foster student engagement in scientific areas. For elementary school students this might mean looking at and identifying natural elements in designs inspired by Marvel's *Black Panther* comics and the film. In chapter 2 middle school students explore cyborg design to build their understanding of biomechanics. High school students can link kinetics to wearable technologies from *Black Panther* that absorb and convert kinetic energy, then use physical prototypes to solve problems.

The integration of culturally relevant making and STEAM learning requires inquiry, collaboration, and emphasis on project- and process-based learning. It also requires a commitment and willingness to include cultural practices and artworks as part of making and STEAM curricular frameworks. The examples discussed in this chapter and throughout the book make intentional connections between personally and culturally relevant artifacts, art and technology, and lesson and project design and implementation. The purpose of the book is to give voice to practitioners from underrepresented ethnic groups that involve TVC modes, to amplify their work in the mainstream maker and STEAM space, and to use this work to inspire and motivate students who might not otherwise know about or be engaged in making.

Conclusion: Building a Culturally Relevant Maker Tool Kit

At the 2018 Literacy Is Liberation Conference, dozens of Boston-area youth gathered at Northeastern University to learn about the connections among Marvel's *Black Panther* film, Afrofuturism, and technology. Many of the young people present were African American and Latino/a. To show more of their representation in STEAM, the presentation focused on the character Shuri who is the princess of a fictional African country called Wakanda and the sister of T'Challa, the Black Panther. As the lead inventor of the Wakandan Design Group, the country's scientific division, Shuri is seen as an innovator who creates much of the country's modern technology. She is perhaps best known for designing the current generation of Panther Habits (superhero suits).

The presentation highlighted some of Shuri's inventions, such as the kimoyo beads that are given to each baby and that provide vast medical knowledge. Other beads, the presentation also showed, have other purposes, including communication and vehicle control. The beads are an example of wearable technology, which is not limited to fiction. The attendees saw a Black Panther–inspired shoe with an embedded pressure sensor that, when pressed, lights up several LEDs similar to light-up sneakers that many young people wear. The shoe was created in a local fab lab as an example of what is possible through digital fabrication. At the conclusion of the workshop, youths were asked how many real-life Shuris they know. Not one hand was raised.

African American, Latino/a, and Indigenous youth struggle to iden-tify a Shuri innovator in their schools and communities for several reasons. In the workforce, science and engineering norms are in conflict with the goals, values, and needs articulated by members of underrepresented ethnic groups, leading them to feel that they do not fit in science and engineering spaces (Cherwitz 2005). Students can pick up on often-subconscious messages about what scientists or engineers look like, value, and do (A. Johnson 2007). Teachers may experience discomfort when asked to recognize student iden-tities as being comparable with "scientist" or "engineer," leaving teachers vulnerable to perpetuating stereotypes about the students' capabilities. TVC provides a clear rationale for integrating making into existing educational frameworks, and Shuri, as a TVC practitio-ner, is one example: she has access, she has the keys to the lab, and she feels welcome.

Because of the success of *Black Panther* and the popularity of Shuri, several articles were written to cover the history and impor-tance of the character. Writers and critics prophesied that Shuri would have a lasting effect on Black girls, inspiring them to pursue STEAM fields after seeing a Black girl innovator. One writer noted, "If I had seen Shuri in this film as a child, I would have wanted to join a coding class right away and develop my own technology group" (Broadnax 2018). Only time will tell how many girls were inspired by Shuri to join STEAM fields. Until then, the lack of real-world professionals from underrepresented ethnic groups in STEM fields is still having a negative effect on young people from these groups (Funk and Parker 2018).

This book provides a culturally relevant making and design tool kit that includes taxonomy for different cultural practices and learning strategies. The modularity of the tools invite adaptation from teachers who work with students from diverse cultures and backgrounds. Teachers can introduce a challenging concept or problem to their students using a design process that includes creating a concept map or using cards with prompts to help students make connections to what they know and what they need to learn. As part of the mapping process, students learn about inventions such as Eye-Writer used by Tempt1 (figure 8.1). Students can unpack the innovation that went into the creation of EyeWriter, Tempt1's remixing of Chicano-style and New York–style graffiti to create something new, or the development of the Graffiti Analysis tool that visualizes the motions of Tempt1's graffiti making.

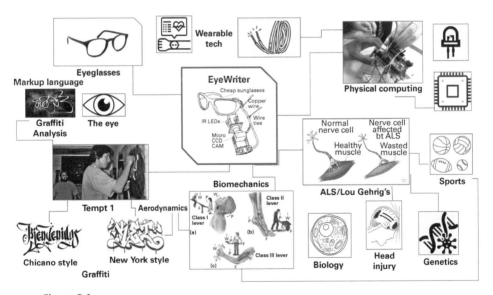

Figure 8.1
Example of an EyeWriter design map as part of a STEAM professional development workshop presentation for teachers.
Photo: Nettrice Gaskins. Courtesy of Dramatic Results.

The development team for EyeWriter consisted of people with expertise in, for example, graffiti, mechanical and electrical engineering, new media, creative hacking, and coding. As part of professional development training, teachers can learn about and work with experts in these areas to create STEAM curricula. They can learn about and practice developing activities as part of a modular prototyping plan (figure 8.2). The fictional Wakandan Design Group looks like any number of real-life programs, such as Black Girls Code and Google's Code Next, that are focused on cultivating leaders in computer science and engineering from African American, Latino/a, and Indigenous communities. Practitioners involved in these programs bring adaptive expertise to experiences such as the design cypher (see Cooke et al. 2015) that is mentioned throughout this book.

Using *Black Panther* props, EyeWriter, and other inventions as examples, teachers can develop plans for projects that address

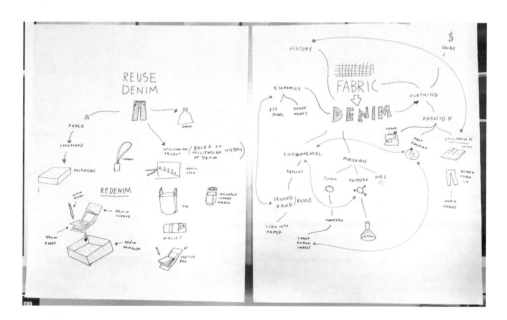

Figure 8.2
A design map created by teachers participating in the STEAM workshop at Dramatic Results in Long Beach, California.
Photo: Nettrice Gaskins. Courtesy of Dramatic Results.

students' interests, persistent social issues, or a community need. This approach is part of inquiry-based instruction, which begins by posing questions, problems, or scenarios, such as exploring the term *self-concept*, which refers to how young people think about, evaluate, or perceive themselves, especially in challenging subjects or areas. Teachers can collect and use a combination of inventions and cultural artifacts to make an initial modular learning prototype. This prototype can be used as the model when teaching students. Prototyping can also be applied to lesson plan development. Teachers can remix existing lesson components to redesign curricula if previous ones prove ineffective.

The challenge with TVC projects is figuring out how to implement them in traditional school settings, especially given time constraints and limited materials. TVC modalities are no different from maker ones in that they require access, time, and space. Districts need to support teachers in the integration of tools in the following ways: encourage experimentation and innovation among teachers and students, invest in tools and technology for use in schools, and make sure that people with expertise are on-site and available. Under-resourced schools can work with college or university STEAM programs and companies such as Autodesk to provide training to teachers, as well as hardware and expertise. Scaling a Community of Practice for Education in STEM through Digital Fabrication, or SCOPES-DF, and similar programs provide a web-based platform where teachers can create, share, and remix lessons.

New Habits, Projects, and Methods

Integrating new strategies and approaches in STEAM education takes time, as does broadening maker educational practices that take place within and outside formal learning settings. Educators can begin with fostering TVC habits of mind that include modulating, translating (decoding), patterning, repeating, combining, and encoding and then applying one or more of these practices in the development of maker or STEAM projects. This is not to assert that there are only six ways in which underrepresented ethnic practitioners display their knowledge. These habits often build on each other and may require further elaboration.

Modulating (funk)

TVC practitioners constantly adapt their work to new situations by responding to other people, artifacts, and the environment. They salvage, repurpose, and transform things that already exist and put them into new contexts. They make maps using seemingly dissimilar ideas and designs. They sample parts of an existing composition, rhythm, or sequence. They layer, adjust, loop, and otherwise manipulate physical and digital artifacts. They reacquire things, break them apart, and remake them to meet a need or solve a problem.

Onyx Ashanti's BeatJazz system combined elements of jazz and hip-hop improvisation, computation, and digital fabrication to make an interface for embodied interaction. Aspects of this system can reinforce engineering design concepts such as inquiry, brainstorming, planning, designing and building, and iteration. Using Ashanti's example, students should be able to come up with designs that reflect a need or interest, including specified criteria and constraints. They can break down a system (or device) into smaller parts, which can be independently created, modified, replaced, or exchanged between different systems.

Translating (decoding)

TVC practitioners convert everyday things into different formats that are useful for new processes. They insist on following a nonlinear path. They interrupt established rhythmic patterns and skip back and forth in time to continue a beat. They make use of formal designs but do not submit to them. They assert change over disciplined order. They transform dominant ideas into locally relevant and responsive designs. They act on what is fixed or constant to make things that are flexible, cyclical, or dynamic.

Indigenous performers such as A Tribe Called Red and hoop dancers convert cultural artifacts—for example, the Native American Medicine Wheel—into performances and installations that engage their communities. These examples can be used to help students convert performance information into kinetics (physics) to show relationships between motions and causes (e.g., forces and torques). Students can explore the kinesthetics (motion) in their performances by making and using a photogate device, which uses a beam of light to measure the time an object is at a certain position.

Encoding

TVC practitioners use alteration or adaptation to redeploy the material and symbolic power of cultural artifacts. They embed cultural symbols and rituals in the things they make. They conceal the meanings of their work from the unaware and unknowing. They mask cultural representations in work meant for mainstream use. They abstract machine-generated artifacts into a polyrhythmic structure or interface. Their works convert speculative concepts into different forms of social or political action.

Artworks that on their surface seem decorative can have deeper meanings. Inquiry-based methods uncover these meanings, showing the artist's intention to embed STEAM concepts in the work. For example, Sanford Biggers repurposes cultural artifacts such as the Buddhist Mandala and break dance cypher. His "Lotus" diagram and similar designs feature cosmograms that are drawn with mathematical roulette curves like a spirograph or using Fibonacci patterns based on a series of numbers. Teachers can use Biggers's designs to demonstrate the main types of geometric transformations: translation, rotation, reflection, and dilation.

Patterning

TVC practitioners often draw on two or more different structural elements simultaneously. They put together differently made sounds or images to add more complexity to a project. They find and use designs that already exist or are overlooked. They have a deep understanding of rhythm sequences. They sustain visual and aural rhythms or beats in distinctive ways to draw people into their work. They can cut in between parts of a song or visual design to create anticipation, indicate the start of a new part, or give an arrangement variety.

Nontsikelelo Mutiti draws on her knowledge of braiding as a way to create complex patterns using black hair combs, tiles, and the y-shaped plaits that make up cornrows. Through physical and digital manipulation, she repeats these objects multiple times to make different patterns. Her work can show students how to perform operations (e.g., design shape patterns based on rules), practice algebraic thinking, and use geometric properties such as rotation, reflection, and translation. Using a grid they can identify the patterns in Mutiti's braided designs, number the motifs, and express these numbers algebraically.

Repeating

TVC practitioners circulate and replicate modules over and over to create and manipulate patterns to make new things. They perform or make things that perform in cyclical or looping patterns. They use call-and-response participation to iterate on existing works. They reiterate the rhythm, interval, scale, and proportion of artifacts. Their temporal and spatial works invite looping and variation, similar to a jazz or rap producer's approach to making songs.

The repetitive rhythmic patterns in funk music (e.g., "Cold Sweat") are amenable to algorithmic design, and these patterns are replicated in hip-hop techniques. For example, Grandmaster Flash's quick mix repeats, on a loop, parts of songs that build up audience anticipation.

His torque theory (mentioned in chapter 1) involved marking records to indicate the "get down" parts of a song. Students can practice these techniques by building their own control boxes or audio mixers and use a MIDI interface to play music using different sounds. This helps students gather digital resources using various tools and methods to make music.

Combining

TVC practitioners invent things by combining elements that nobody else thought to put together. They layer, merge, or collage different forms, materials, and sources to make new things, putting them together in such a way that each move in a work determines a subsequent action or response. They gather all the ingredients together and allow them to logically coalesce into something more than the sum of their parts. Their works are hybrids, existing in more than one discipline or domain.

Guillermo Bert's "La Bestia" combines Indigenous heritage artifacts and digital fabrication (laser cutting) with QR codes (2D bar codes) to access information and sustain the oral traditions of storytelling. This work can help students communicate clearly and express themselves creatively using platforms, tools, and digital media. Students can combine electronic devices such as Makey Makeys with block-based visual programming tools to trigger stories. The Makey Makey replaces the computer keyboard and acts as a storytelling "interface."

Some Closing Words

The descriptions for TVC habits of mind, artworks, and learning methods are drawn from research on culturally relevant making in underrepresented ethnic communities. When addressing a problem, practitioners from these communities routinely use one or more of these habits. The list serves as a starting point for further elaboration and description. TVC habits of mind cover all subjects commonly taught in schools, adding additional layers of meaning and intention to materials teachers use and methods that are implemented in classrooms and labs. The goal of STEAM education therefore should be to support students in liberating, developing, and adopting TVC habits of mind more fully. Taken together, they are a force directing us toward increasingly authentic, relevant, and equitable actions.

TVC is where STEAM learning takes place. TVC modes govern how students learn, and they form a framework for engagement that centers the everyday experiences and practices of underrepresented ethnic groups. Educators can use TVC habits to distinguish fundamental questions, ideas, and deliverables regarding strategies

Figure 8.3
Techno-vernacular creativity. © Tamra Carhart 2020 (https://carhartcreative.com).

for engaging underrepresented ethnic learners in STEAM. Educators can use the modular qualities of TVC activities to design curricula—for instance, one that merges math, computation, and design. Although it may take more work and funding, it is essential to make connections between what needs to be taught in school and what could make the experience of teaching and learning more relevant to those who feel the least connected.

Afterword

Ruha Benjamin

In April 2020, as the COVID-19 crisis deepened, a group of young people in Boston's South End neighborhood launched a campaign to distribute personal protective equipment (PPE) to frontline workers, the elderly, homeless people, and other community members most vulnerable to exposure. Because of the US federal government's notoriously weak pandemic response, not even those who worked in the city's hospitals and clinics had the supplies they needed. In collaboration with the Party for Socialism and Liberation, Boston teens launched PPE for the People, creating hundreds of cloth masks, face shields, and N95 respirators using sewing machines, laser cutters, and 3D printing machines at the South End Technology Center. Incorporating safety and style, they fabricated PPE with vibrant colors and African prints, exemplifying the kind of inventiveness and creativity that Nettrice Gaskins powerfully theorizes in the preceding pages. Like her analysis, the PPE campaign showcases young people's *ingenuity* even as it highlights the broader-context *inequity*—why should teens be the ones safeguarding public health in the first place?

The civil rights activist and politician Mel King founded the South End Technology Center at Tent City in 2002, offering free tutoring, computer courses, and training on how to use the equipment in the fab lab. "I want people to tell their story their way, unabridged," King says—a vision that also animates this book. Yet everywhere we turn, technology is used not only to distort people's stories but to actively discriminate against already dispossessed groups, albeit in more coded form, but not without resistance.

In November 2018, high school students in Brooklyn, New York, staged a walkout to protest their school's adoption of a Facebook-designed online program that promised "personalized learning," "self-direction," and "working at your own pace." But with only ten to fifteen minutes of one-on-one "mentoring" from a teacher each week, the students called bullshit on all the buzzwords. "We have to teach ourselves," one explained. It turns out, staring at a screen all day is exhausting and distracting, and it's easy to cheat and get good grades without really learning, so lamented the students.

A year earlier, parents, students, and community members in St. Paul, Minnesota, rallied against a new city program called the Innovation Project, which launched a joint powers agreement between the public schools and police department giving these agencies broad discretion to collect and share data on young people with the goal of developing predictive tools to identify at-risk youth in the city. There was immediate and broad-based backlash from the community, and a group of over twenty local organizations formed the Stop the Cradle to Prison Algorithm Coalition, eventually shutting down the project in favor of a more community-led approach.

In August 2020, thousands of young people across the United Kingdom flooded the streets in protest of an automated grading system; "Algorithm Elitism!" "Teachers Really *Know*, Computer Grades *Must Go!*" "Your Algorithm Doesn't Know Me!" read their posters. Given the COVID pandemic, students were unable to take the usual high-stakes secondary school exam, which determines what universities they are eligible to attend. So the government Office of Qualifications and Examinations Regulation (Ofqual) produced algorithmically generated scores with the aim of moderating teachers' grade predictions and curbing grade inflation. What could possibly go wrong?

When the results were released, widespread public outcry focused on the downgrading of scores for public school students and upgrading of results for those attending private schools. Who could've predicted? Although officials initially held fast to the results, saying they were "robust and dependable" and that there would be "no U-turn, no change," after two days of massive protests and legal action, Ofqual and the secretary of education backed down. The algorithmically derived scores would be dropped and, as a result, the number of top grades increased dramatically.

The first lesson in all of this, of course, is that *protest works*. Young people and their advocates are standing up to the techno–status quo, refusing to be objectified by algorithms, and demanding the right to shape their own futures. The second lesson is that technologies are always poised to reinforce unjust power dynamics, unless those who have historically been disempowered are able to fully imagine and craft what tools are deemed necessary in the first place.

The Ofqual grading controversy and PPE for the People campaign are two sides of technology's split screen. The former represents what I term *engineered inequity*—top-down systems designed to create social distinctions and hierarchies. The latter, by contrast, exemplifies Nettrice Gaskins's incisive framework of *techno-vernacular creativity*—culturally situated innovations that are often overlooked. The question now is, which version of technology will we allow to propagate?

The famed black feminist writer Audre Lorde is often quoted as saying, "The master's tools will never dismantle the master's house." But what if we're not interested in dismantling his house? After all, it seems to be burning down quite well on its own. Instead, what if we want to build our own house? In these pages, we find conceptual tools and cultural blueprints that take us beyond critique of technology to creative praxis, which we can use to construct a world that is more just and joyful than the deadly structures we currently inhabit.

References

Abrahamson, Dor, and Robb Lindgren. 2014. "Embodiment and Embodied Design." In *The Cambridge Handbook of the Learning Sciences*, 2nd ed., edited by R. Keith Sawyer, 358–376. Cambridge: Cambridge University Press.

Adebayo, Binwe. 2017. "RUKA: Blending URL and IRL with Zimbabwean Artist Nontsikelelo Mutiti." *Bubblegum Club*. https://bubblegumclub.co.za /art-and-culture/ruka-blending-url-irl-zimbabwean-artist-nontsikelelo -mutiti.

Alexander, Stephon. 2017. *The Jazz of Physics: The Secret Link between Music and the Structure of the Universe*. New York: Basic Books.

Allina, Babette. 2018. "The Development of STEAM Educational Policy to Promote Student Creativity and Social Empowerment." *Arts Education Policy Review* 119 (2): 77–87.

Anderson, Maria. 2017. "A Lesson in 'Rasquachismo' Art: Chicano Aesthetics & the 'Sensibilities of the Barrio.'" *Smithsonian Insider*, January 31. https://insider.si.edu/2017/01/lesson-rasquachismo-chicano-asthetics -taste-underdog.

Anderson, Reynaldo. 2016. "Afrofuturism 2.0 and the Black Speculative Art Movement: Notes on a Manifesto." *How We Get to Next*, January 22. https://howwegettonext.com/afrofuturism-2-0-and-the-black-speculative -art-movement-notes-on-a-manifesto-f4e2ae6b3b4d.

Andreae, Christopher. 2004. "Bearden Created the Visual Equivalent of Jazz." *Christian Science Monitor,* October 4. https://www.csmonitor.com /2004/1004/p18s02-hfes.html.

Archer, Louise, Emily Dawson, Jennifer Dewitt, Amy Seakins, and Billy Wong. 2015. "'Science Capital': A Conceptual, Methodological, and Empirical Argument for Extending Bourdieusian Notions of Capital beyond the Arts." *Journal of Research in Science Teaching* 52 (7): 922–948.

Arnone, Marilyn, Ruth Small, Sarah Chauncey, and Patricia H. McKenna. 2011. "Curiosity, Interest and Engagement in Technology-Pervasive Learning Environments: A New Research Agenda." *Educational Technology Research and Development* 59 (2): 181–198.

Auger, James. 2013. "Speculative Design: Crafting the Speculation." *Digital Creativity* 24 (1): 11–35.

B3R3Z1N4. 2008. "Wild Style (Doze)." YouTube video, 06:17. November 16. https://www.youtube.com/watch?v=ZyK20wFamQw.

Baatjes, Ivor. 2003. "The New Knowledge-Rich Society: Perpetuating Marginalisation and Exclusion." *Journal of Education,* no. 29: 179–204.

Babbitt, Bill, Dan Lyles, and Ron Eglash. 2012. "From Ethnomathematics to Ethnocomputing." In *Alternative Forms of Knowing in Mathematics: Celebrations of Diversity of Mathematical Practices,* edited by Swapna Mukhopadhyay and Wolff-Michael Roth, 205–220. Rotterdam, Netherlands: Sense.

Bales, Judy. 2012. "Creating Again and Again: Fractal Patterns and Process in Improvisational African-American Quilts." *Critical Interventions* 6 (1): 63–83.

Banks, Adam J. 2011. *Digital Griots: African American Rhetoric in a Multimedia Age.* Carbondale: Southern Illinois University Press.

Baraka, Amiri. 1971. "Technology & Ethos." In *Raise, Race, Rays, Raze: Essays since 1965,* 155–156. New York: Random House.

Bare Conductive. 2020. "Q&A: Art and Decibels by Thomas Evans." Accessed October 6. https://www.bareconductive.com/news/qa-art-and-decibels-by -thomas-evans.

Bartlett, Andrew. 1994. "Airshafts, Loudspeakers, and the Hip Hop Sample: Contexts and African American Musical Aesthetics." *African American Review* 28 (4): 639–652.

Bayram, Zeki, Özge Oskay, Emine Erdem, Sinem Dinçol Özgür, and Şenol Şen. 2013. "Effect of Inquiry Based Learning Method on Students' Motivation." *Procedia—Social and Behavioral Sciences* 106:988–996.

Bennett, Audrey. 2016. "Ethnocomputational Creativity in STEAM Education: A Cultural Framework for Generative Justice." *Revista Teknokultura* 13 (2): 587–612.

Blikstein, Paulo. 2008. "Travels in Troy with Freire: Technology as an Agent for Emancipation." In *Social Justice Education for Teachers: Paulo Freire and the Possible Dream*, edited by Pedro Noguera and Carlos Alberto Torres, 205–244. Rotterdam, Netherlands: Sense.

Blikstein, Paulo. 2013. "Digital Fabrication and 'Making' in Education: The Democratization of Invention." In *FabLabs: Of Machines, Makers and Inventors*, edited by Corinne Büching and Julia Walter-Herrmann, 203–222. Bielefeld, Germany: Transcript Publishers.

Broadnax, Jamie. 2018. "Everyone Loves Shuri: The History and Importance of Marvel's Teenage Tech Genius." *Lily*, February 25. https://www.thelily.com/everyone-loves-shuri-the-history-and-importance-of-marvels-teenage-tech-genius.

Brown, John Seely, and Paul Duguid. 1991. "Organizational Learning and Communities-of-Practice: Toward a Unified View of Working, Learning, and Innovation." *Organization Science* 2:40–57.

Buechley, Leah. 2013. "Thinking about Making." Speech delivered at the FabLearn Conference, Stanford, CA, October 27–28.

Buechley, Leah. 2014. "Eyeo 2014." Vimeo. https://vimeo.com/110616469.

Burgess, Phillip. 2014. "UNTZtrument: A Trellis MIDI Instrument." *Adafruit*, June 20. https://learn.adafruit.com/untztrument-trellis-midi-instrument.

Calabrese Barton, Angela, and Edna Tan. 2018. "A Longitudinal Study of Equity-Oriented STEM-Rich Making among Youth from Historically Marginalized Communities." *American Educational Research Journal* 55 (4): 761–800.

Castillo, Michelle. 2011. "Study: This Is Your Brain on Improv." *Time*, January 20.

Chappell, Ben. 2014. *Lowrider Space Aesthetics and Politics of Mexican American Custom Cars*. Austin: University of Texas Press.

Cheliotis, Giorgos, and Jude Yew. 2009. "An Analysis of the Social Structure of Remix Culture." In *Proceedings of the Fourth International Conference on Communities and Technologies*, edited by John M. Carroll, 165–174. New York: Association for Computing Machinery.

Cherwitz, Richard A. 2005. "Diversifying Graduate Education: The Promise of Intellectual Entrepreneurship." *Journal of Hispanic Higher Education* 4 (1): 19–33.

Chiefs for Change. 2019. *Honoring Origins and Helping Students Succeed: The Case for Cultural Relevance in High-Quality Instructional Materials.* Washington, DC: Chiefs for Change.

Coleman, Beth. 2009. "Race as Technology." *Camera Obscura* 24 (1 (70)): 177–207.

Cooke, Sekou, Olalekan Jeyifous, Rashida Bumbray, Michael Ford, Andres L. Hernandez, Craig L. Wilkins, Lawrence Chua, et al. 2015. "Towards a Hip-Hop Architecture." Syracuse University School of Architecture 194. https://surface.syr.edu/arc/194.

Daley, Barbara J. "Using Concept Maps in Qualitative Research." In *Concept Maps: Theory, Methodology, Technology; Proceedings of the First International Conference on Concept Mapping*, vol. 1, edited by Alberto J. Cañas, Joseph D. Novak, and Fermin M. González, 191–197. Pamplona, Spain: Universidad Pública de Navarra.

Dasgupta, Sayamindu, William Hale, Andrés Monroy-Hernández, and Benjamin Mako Hill. 2016. "Remixing as a Pathway to Computational Thinking." In *CSCW '16: Proceedings of the 19th ACM Conference on Computer-Supported Cooperative Work & Social Computing*, 1438–1449. New York: Association for Computing Machinery.

de Brey, Cristobal, Lauren Musu, Joel McFarland, Sidney Wilkinson-Flicker, Melissa Diliberti, Anlan Zhang, et al. 2019. *Status and Trends in the Education of Racial and Ethnic Groups 2018*. US Department of Education, Institute of Education Sciences, National Center for Education Statistics.

Dery, Mark. 1994. *Flame Wars: The Discourse of Cyberculture*. Durham, NC: Duke University Press.

Desowitz, Bill. 2018. "'Black Panther': How Wakanda Got a Written Language as Part of Its Afrofuturism." *Indiewire*, February 22. https://www

.indiewire.com/2018/02/black-panther-wakanda-written-language-ryan
-coogler-afrofuturism-1201931252.

De Spain, Kent. 2003. "The Cutting Edge of Awareness: Reports from the Inside of Improvisation." In *Taken by Surprise: A Dance Improvisation Reader*, edited by Ann Cooper Albright, 27–38. Middletown, CT: Wesleyan University Press.

Dewey, John. (1897) 1940. "My Pedagogic Creed." In *The School Journal* 54:77–80.

Dillon, Grace. 2012. *Walking the Clouds: An Anthology of Indigenous Science Fiction*. Tucson: University of Arizona Press.

Dixon, Brent Ritchie. 2015. "Technological Doodling as a Learning and Design Practice." PhD diss., University of Texas at Austin.

Dolberry, Maurice E. 2015. "From 'They' Science to 'Our' Science: Hip Hop Epistemology in STEAM Education." PhD diss., University of Washington.

Dooley, Tatum. 2019. "Stephanie Dinkins Is Turning Memoir into AI." *Garage*, August 15. https://garage.vice.com/en_us/article/43kdnm/stephanie -dinkins-is-turning-memoir-into-ai.

d'Orléans, Paul. 2014. *The Chopper: The Real Story*. New York: Gestalten.

Du Bois, W. E. B. (1905) 2015. "The Princess Steel." *PMLA* 130 (3): 819–829.

Dunne, Anthony, and Fiona Raby. 2014. *Speculative Everything: Design, Fiction, and Social Dreaming*. Cambridge, MA: MIT Press.

Eglash, Ron. 1999. *African Fractals: Modern Computing and Indigenous Design*. New Brunswick, NJ: Rutgers University Press.

Eglash, Ron. 2004. "A Geometric Bridge Across the Middle Passage: Mathematics in the Art of John Biggers." *International Review of African American Art* 19 (3): 28–33.

Eglash, Ron, Audrey Bennett, Casey O'Donnell, Sybillyn Jennings, and Margaret Cintorino. 2006. "Culturally Situated Design Tools: Ethnocomputing from Field Site to Classroom." *American Anthropologist* 108 (2): 347–362.

Eglash, Ron, and Ellen Foster. 2014. "On the Politics of Generative Justice: African Traditions and Maker Communities." Paper presented at the conference "What Do Science, Technology, and Innovation Mean from Africa?," MIT, Cambridge, MA, November 13–15.

Eglash, Ron, and Colin Garvey. 2014. "Basins of Attraction for Generative Justice." In *Chaos Theory in Politics*, edited by Santo Banerjee, Şefika Şule Erçetin, and Ali Tekin, 75–88. Dordrecht, Netherlands: Springer Science & Business Media.

Elkordy, Angela, and Ayn F. Keneman. 2019. *Design Ed: Connecting Learning Science Research to Practice*. Portland, OR: International Society for Technology in Education.

El-Zanfaly, Dina. 2015. "[I3] Imitation, Iteration and Improvisation: Embodied Interaction in Making and Learning." *Design Studies* 41 (Part A): 79–109.

Emdin, Christopher. 2007. "Exploring the Contexts of Urban Science Classrooms. Part 1: Investigating Corporate and Communal Practices." *Cultural Studies of Science Education* 2 (2): 319–350.

Emdin, Christopher. 2010. *Urban Science Education for the Hip-Hop Generation*. Rotterdam, Netherlands: Sense.

Emdin, Christopher, and Edmund S. Adjapong. 2018. *#HipHopEd: The Compilation on Hip-hop Education*, vol. 1, *Hip-hop as Education, Philosophy, and Practice*. Leiden, Netherlands: Brill.

Estabrooks, Leigh B., and Stephanie R. Couch. 2018 "Failure as an Active Agent in the Development of Creative and Inventive Mindsets." *Thinking Skills and Creativity* 30:103–115.

Falk, John H. 2003. "Personal Meaning Mapping." In *Museums and Creativity: A Study into the Role of Museums in Design Education*, edited by Geoffrey Caban, John H. Falk, Lynn D. Dierking, and Carol Scott, 10–18. Sydney: Powerhouse.

Falk, John H., and Martin Storksdieck. 2005. "Using the Contextual Model of Learning to Understand Visitor Learning from a Science Center Exhibition." *Science Education* 89:744–778.

Fassler, Joe. 2013. "All Immigrants Are Artists." *Atlantic*, August 27. https://www.theatlantic.com/entertainment/archive/2013/08/all-immigrants-are-artists/279087.

Fouché, Rayvon. 2006. "Say It Loud, I'm Black and I'm Proud: African Americans, American Artifactual Culture, and Black Vernacular Technological Creativity." *American Quarterly* 58 (3): 639–661.

Funk, Cary, and Kim Parker. 2018. "Women and Men in STEM Often at Odds over Workplace Equity." *Pew Research Center*, January 9. https://www .pewsocialtrends.org/2018/01/09/women-and-men-in-stem-often-at-odds -over-workplace-equity.

Gab, Shari. 2016. "A Brief History of Automotive Hydraulics." *InsideHook*, June 20. https://www.insidehook.com/article/vehicles/a-brief-history-of-auto motive-hydraulics.

Gaskins, Nettrice. 2014. "Techno-Vernacular Creativity & Innovation in Underrepresented Communities of Practice." PhD diss., Georgia Institute of Technology.

Gaskins, Nettrice. 2016. "The African Cosmogram Matrix in Contemporary Art and Culture." *Black Theology* 14 (1): 28–42.

Gaskins, Nettrice. 2017. "Machine Drawing: Shantell Martin and the Algorist." *Art21 Magazine*, July 6. http://magazine.art21.org/2017/07/06/mach ine-drawing-shantell-martin-and-the-algorist/#.XM429mRKi2x.

Georgas, Helen, Mariana Regalado, and Matthew Burgess. 2017. "Choose Your Own Adventure: The Hero's Journey and the Research Process." In *Association of College & Research Libraries Conference 2017 Proceedings*, edited by Dawn M. Mueller, 120–132. Chicago.

George, Nelson, Sally Banes, Susan Flinker, and Patty Romanowski. 1985. *Fresh: Hip-Hop Don't Stop*. New York: Random House.

Godrej, Farah. 2011. "Spaces for Counter-Narratives: The Phenomenology of Reclamation." *Frontiers: A Journal of Women Studies* 32 (3): 111–133.

Goeman, Mishuana. 2013. *Mark My Words: Native Women Mapping Our Nations*. Minneapolis: University of Minnesota Press.

Gomes, Patrícia. 2016. "'Diversity Does Not Happen by Accident' and Other Lessons about Equity in the Maker Movement." *EdSurge*, May 11. https://www.edsurge.com/news/2016-05-11-diversity-does-not-happen-by - accident-and-other-lessons-about-equity-in-the-maker-movement.

Graves, Jen. 2011. "The Supernaturalist: Xenobia Bailey and How She Got That Way." *The Stranger*, November 16. https://www.thestranger.com/seattle /the-supernaturalist/Content?oid=10729199.

Guestlistener. 2014. "A Tribe Called Red Remixes Sonic Stereotypes." *Sounding Out!*, February 13. https://soundstudiesblog.com/2014/02/13/a-tribe-call ed-red-remixes-sonic-stereotypes.

Hagerman, Michelle S., and Megan Cotnam-Kappel. 2019. "Making as Embodied Learning: Rethinking the Importance of Movement for Learning with Digital and Physical Tools." *Education Review* 6 (2): 1–3.

Hatano, Giyoo, and Yoko Oura. 2003. "Commentary: Reconceptualizing School Learning Using Insight from Expertise Research." *Educational Researcher* 32 (8): 26–29.

Henriques, Julian. 2011. *Sonic Bodies: Reggae Sound Systems, Performance Techniques, and Ways of Knowing.* New York: Continuum.

Ho Chu, Jean, Paul Clifton, Daniel Harley, Jordanne Pavao, and Ali Mazalek. 2015. "Mapping Place: Supporting Cultural Learning through a Lukasa-Inspired Tangible Tabletop Museum Exhibit." In *TEI 2015—Proceedings of the 9th International Conference on Tangible, Embedded, and Embodied Interaction,* edited by Bill Verplank, 261–268. New York: Association for Computing Machinery.

hooks, bell. 1995. "Black Vernacular: Architecture as Cultural Practice." In *Art on My Mind: Visual Politics,* 145–151. New York: New Press.

Irvine, Martin. 2014. "Remix and the Dialogic Engine of Culture: A Model for Generative Combinatoriality." In *The Routledge Companion to Remix Studies,* edited by Owen Gallagher, Eduardo Navas, and Xtine Burrough, 15–42. New York: Routledge.

Itō, Mizuko, Sonja Baumer, and Matteo Bittanti. 2019. *Hanging Out, Messing Around, and Geeking Out: Kids Living and Learning with New Media.* Cambridge, MA: MIT Press.

Iyer, Vijay. 2002. "Embodied Mind, Situated Cognition, and Expressive Microtiming in African-American Music." *Music Perception: An Interdisciplinary Journal* 19 (3): 387–414.

Johnson, Angela C. 2007. "Unintended Consequences: How Science Professors Discourage Women of Color." *Science Education* 91 (5): 805–821.

Johnson, Cecilia. 2017. "Roger Linn, Inventor of the LM-1 Drum Machine, Talks Prince and 'When Doves Cry.'" https://www.thecurrent.org/feature/2017/03/01/roger-linn-inventor-of-the-lm1-drum-machine-talks-prince-and-when-doves-cry.

Johnson, Victoria. 2018. "Breaking Down the Futuristic Technology of 'Black Panther.'" *Mashable,* March 1. https://mashable.com/2018/03/01/black-panther-technology.

Kafai, Yasmin B., and Quinn Burke. 2016. *Connected Code: Why Children Need to Learn Programming*. Cambridge, MA: MIT Press.

Kafai, Yasmin, Deborah Fields, and Kristin Searle. 2014. "Electronic Textiles as Disruptive Designs: Supporting and Challenging Maker Activities in Schools." *Harvard Educational Review* 84 (4): 532–556.

Kamkwamba, William, and Bryan Mealer. 2010. *The Boy Who Harnessed the Wind: A Memoir*. London: HarperTrue.

Kanellos, Nicolas. 1994. *Handbook of Hispanic Cultures in the United States: Anthropology*. Houston: Arte Publico.

Kaufman, James C., and Ronald A. Beghetto. 2019. "Beyond Big and Little: The Four C Model of Creativity." *Review of General Psychology* 13:1–12.

Keller, John. 2010. *Motivational Design for Learning and Performance: The ARCS Model Approach*. New York: Springer.

Kim, Daniel. 2015. "Future Visions: Technology and Citizenship in Underwater Dreams." *Technology and Culture* 56 (2): 530–532.

Klimczak, Susan. 2016. "Technologies of the Heart: Beyond #BlackLivesMatter and toward #MakingLiberation." In *Meaningful Making: Projects and Inspirations for Fab Labs Makerspaces*, edited by Paulo Blikstein, Sylvia Libow Martinez, and Heather Allen Pang, 61–67. Torrance, CA: Constructing Modern Knowledge Press.

Knight, Terry. 2018. "Craft, Performance, and Grammars." In *Computational Studies on Cultural Variation and Heredity*, 205–224. Daejeon, South Korea: KAIST.

Knight, Terry, and George Stiny. 2015. "Making Grammars: From Computing with Shapes to Computing with Things." *Design Studies* 41 (Part A): 8–28.

Lachney, Michael. 2017. "Computational Communities: African American Cultural Capital in Computer Science Education." *Computer Science Education* 27 (3–4): 175–196.

Landgraf, Edgar. 2014. *Improvisation as Art: Conceptual Challenges, Historical Perspectives*. London: Bloomsbury.

Landry, Lauren. 2012. "15-Year-Old, Self-Taught Engineer Wows the MIT Media Lab." *BostInno*. November 20. https://www.americaninno.com/boston/kelvin-doe-vide-youngest-student-at-the-mit-media-lab/#ss2619 11_170540_0ss.

Lave, Jean, and Etienne Wenger. 1991. *Situated Learning: Legitimate Peripheral Participation*. Cambridge: Cambridge University Press.

Lee, Carol D. 2001. "Is October Brown Chinese: A Cultural Modeling Activity System for Underachieving Students." *American Educational Research Journal* 38 (1): 97–142.

Leon, Eli. 1998. *No Two Alike: African-American Improvisations on a Traditional Patchwork Pattern*. Columbia: South Carolina State Museum.

Leshnick, Sengsouvanh, Jackie Statum Allen, and Daniela Berman. 2019. "Bridging the Gap: Study Reveals Supports Teachers Need to Move from Understanding to Implementation." *Learning Professional* 40 (4): 36–39.

Levingston, Tobie Gene. 2003. *Soul on Bikes: The East Bay Dragons MC and the Black Biker Set*. Minneapolis, MN: Motorbooks International.

Lévi-Strauss, Claude. 1962. *The Savage Mind*. Chicago: University of Chicago Press.

Lewis, Brooke A. 2017. "Teens Add Their Personalities to Play Area of Houston Housing Complex." *Houston Chronicle*, January 14.

Limb, Charles J., and Allen R. Braun. 2008. "Neural Substrates of Spontaneous Musical Performance: An fMRI Study of Jazz Improvisation." *PLoS ONE* 3 (2). https://journals.plos.org/plosone/article?id=10.1371/journal.pone.000 1679.

Lister, Raymond, Elizabeth Adams, Sue Fitzgerald, William Fone, John Hamer, Morten Lindholm, Robert Mccartney, et al. 2005. "A Multi-national Study of Reading and Tracing Skills in Novice Programmers." *ACM SIGCSE Bulletin* 36:119–150.

Lockford, Lesa, and Ronald J. Pelias. 2004. "Bodily Poeticizing in Theatrical Improvisation: A Typology of Performative Knowledge." *Theatre Topics* 14:431–443.

Love, Bettina L. 2012. *Hip Hop's Li'l Sistas Speak: Negotiating Hip Hop Identities and Politics in the New South*. New York: Peter Lang.

Lubart, Todd I. 2001. "Models of the Creative Process: Past, Present and Future." *Creativity Research Journal* 13 (3–4): 295–308.

Ludigkeit, Dirk. 2001. "Collective Improvisation and Narrative Structure in Toni Morrison's Jazz." *LIT* 12:165–187.

MacDowell, Paula. 2015. "Empowering Girls as Change Makers in Maker Culture: Stories from a Summer Camp for Girls in Design, Media & Technology." PhD diss., University of British Columbia at Vancouver.

Mack, John. 2012. "Making and Seeing: Matisse and the Understanding of Kuba Pattern." *Journal of Art Historiography*, no. 7, December.

Martin, Lee. 2015. "The Promise of the Maker Movement for Education." *Journal of Pre-college Engineering Education Research (J-PEER)* 5 (1), article 4.

Martin, Taylor, Stephanie Baker Peacock, Pat Ko, and Jennifer J. Rudolph. 2015. "Changes in Teachers' Adaptive Expertise in an Engineering Professional Development Course." *Journal of Pre-college Engineering Education Research (J-PEER)* 5 (2), article 4.

Martinez, Sylvia. 2015. "Making for All: How to Build an Inclusive Makerspace." *EdSurge*, May 10. https://www.edsurge.com/news/2015-05-10-making-for-all-how-to-build-an-inclusive-makerspace.

Martinez, Sylvia Libow, and Gary Stager. 2019. *Invent to Learn: Making, Tinkering, and Engineering in the Classroom.* 2nd ed. Torrance, CA: Constructing Modern Knowledge Press.

Mazalek, Alexandra, and Paul Clifton. 2014. "Tangible and Embodied Memory Maps: Design of a Lukasa-Inspired Interactive Exhibit." *Africa Atlanta 2014.* https://leading-edge.iac.gatech.edu/aaproceedings/tangible-and-embodied.

McCluskey, Murton. 1995. *Your Guide to Understanding and Enjoying Pow Wows.* Helena: Montana State Office of Public Instruction.

McDermott, Ray P., and Jason Raley. 2011. "Looking Closely: Toward a Natural History of Human Ingenuity." In *The Sage Handbook of Visual Research Methods*, edited by Luc Pauwels and Eric Margolis, 372–391. London: Sage.

McIntyre, Gina. 2018. "The Bold Costumes of 'Black Panther' Join Tradition and Technology." *Los Angeles Times*, November 7. https://www.latimes.com/entertainment/envelope/la-en-mn-costumes-black-panther-20181107-story.html.

Mejia, Joel A., and Alberto L. Pulido. 2018. "Fregados Pero no Jodidos: A Case Study of Latinx Rasquachismo." In *Proceedings American Society for Engineering Education (ASEE) Annual Conference.* Salt Lake City: American Society for

Engineering Education. https://www.asee.org/public/conferences/106/papers/22678/view.

Mercier, Emma M., and Steven E. Higgins. 2013. "Collaborative Learning with Multi-touch Technology: Developing Adaptive Expertise." *Learning and Instruction* 25:13–23.

Moore, Roxanne, Meltem Alemdar, Sunni Haag Newton, and Anna Newsome Holcomb. 2017. "The K–12 InVenture Challenge: Inspiring Future Innovators and Entrepreneurs." Washington, DC: American Society for Engineering Education.

Murray, Amanda. 2010. "Invention Hot Spot: Birth of Hip-Hop in the Bronx, New York, in the 1970s." *Lemelson Center for the Study of Invention and Innovation*, October 15. http://invention.si.edu/invention-hot-spot-birth-hip-hop-bronx-new-york-1970s.

Nasir, Na'ilah Suad, Ann Roseberry, Beth Warren, and Carol Lee. 2005. "Learning as a Cultural Process: Achieving Equity through Diversity." In *Cambridge Handbook of the Learning Sciences*, edited by R. Keith Sawyer, 489–504. New York: Cambridge University Press.

Nasir, Na'ilah Suad, and Sepehr Vakil. 2017. "STEM-Focused Academies in Urban Schools: Tensions and Possibilities." *Journal of the Learning Sciences* 26 (3): 376–406.

National Science Foundation. 2013. *Advancing STEM through Culturally Situated Arts-Based Learning*. AISL-7556. Alexandria, VA.

National Science Foundation, National Center for Science and Engineering Statistics. 2017. *Women, Minorities, and Persons with Disabilities in Science and Engineering*. Special Report NSF 17-310. Arlington, VA.

Navas, Eduardo. 2012. *Remix Theory: The Aesthetics of Sampling*. New York: Springer Wein.

Nelson, Alondra, and Thuy Linh N. Tu. *Technicolor: Race, Technology, and Everyday Life*. New York: New York University Press, 2001.

Noel, Vernelle A. A. 2015. "The Bailey-Derek Grammar: Recording the Craft of Wire-Bending in the Trinidad Carnival." *Leonardo* 48 (4): 357–365.

Nolan, Ginger. 2015. "Savage Mind to Savage Machine: Techniques and Disciplines of Creativity, c. 1880–1985." PhD diss., Columbia University.

Papert, Seymour. 1980. *Mindstorms: Children, Computers, and Powerful Ideas.* New York: Basic Books.

Papert, Seymour. 1993. *The Children's Machine.* New York: Basic Books.

Przybylla, Mareen, and Ralf Romeike. 2014. "Physical Computing and Its Scope: Towards a Constructionist Computer Science Curriculum with Physical Computing." *Informatics in Education* 13 (2): 241–254.

Quattrocchi, Christina. 2013. "MAKE'ing More Diverse Makers." *EdSurge,* October 29. https://www.edsurge.com/news/2013-10-29-make-ing-more-diverse-makers.

Quintana, Chris, Brian J. Reiser, Elizabeth A. Davis, Joseph Krajcik, Eric Fretz, Ravit Golan Duncan, Eleni Kyza, et al. 2004. "A Scaffolding Design Framework for Software to Support Science Inquiry." *Journal of the Learning Sciences* 13 (3): 337–386.

Rajagopalan, Ramgopal, Eric Hortop, Dania El-Khechen, Cheryl Kolak Dudek, Lydia Sharman, F. László Szabó, Thomas Fevens, and Sudhir P. Mudur. 2006. "Inference and Design in Kuba and Zillij Art with Shape Grammars." In *Bridges London: Proceedings of the 2006 Conference on Mathematical Connections in Art, Music and Science,* edited by Reza Sarhangi and John Sharp, 419–428. London, UK: Tarquin Publications.

Recollet, Karyn. 2016. "Gesturing Indigenous Futurities through the Remix." *Dance Research Journal* 48 (1): 91–105.

Reimann, Daniela. 2011. "Shaping Interactive Media with the Sewing Machine: Smart Textile as an Artistic Context to Engage Girls in Technology and Engineering Education." *International Journal of Art, Culture and Design Technologies* 1 (1): 12–21.

Roberts, Mary N., and Allen F. Roberts, eds. 1996. *Memory: Luba Art and the Making of History.* New York: Museum for African Art.

Rodriguez, Elizabeth. 2014. "Cultural Diversity as Computational Diversity: Software Development for Ethnocomputing." Master's thesis, Rensselaer Polytechnic Institute.

Root-Bernstein, Robert. 2001. "Music, Creativity and Scientific Thinking." *Leonardo* 34 (1): 63–68.

Root-Bernstein, Robert, and Michelle Root-Bernstein. 2013. "The Importance of Early and Persistent Arts and Crafts Education for Future Scientists

and Engineers." *SEAD*. https://seadnetwork.wordpress.com/white-paper
-abstracts/final-white-papers/the-importance-of-early-and-persistent-arts
-and-crafts-education-for-future-scientists-and-engineers.

Rose, Tricia. 1994. *Black Noise: Rap Music and Black Culture in Contemporary America*. Hanover, NH: Wesleyan University Press.

Roth, Evan. 2005. "Geek Graffiti: A Study in Computation, Gesture, and Graffiti Analysis." Master's thesis, Parsons School of Design.

Roussos Maria, Andrew Johnson, Jason Leigh, Craig R. Barnes, Christina A. Vasilakis, and Thomas G. Moher. 1997. "The NICE Project: Narrative, Immersive, Constructionist/Collaborative Environments for Learning in Virtual Reality." In *Proc ED-MEDIA/ED-TELECOM 97*, 917–922. Chicago: University of Illinois.

Rudolph, Adam. 2010. "Music and Mysticism, Rhythm and Form: A Blues Romance in 12 Parts." In *Arcana V: Music, Magic and Mysticism*, edited by John Zorn, 327–335. New York: Distributed Art.

Runcie, Dan. 2018. "Looking Ahead at Rap's Future in Virtual Reality with Lupe Fiasco." *Complex*, March 5. https://www.complex.com/pigeons-and
-planes/2018/03/rap-virtual-reality-future-autodesk-hip-hop-design.

Ryoo, Jean J., Nicole Bulalacao, Linda Kekelis, Emily McLeod, and Ben Henriquez. 2015. "Tinkering with 'Failure': Equity, Learning, and the Iterative Design Process." Paper presented at the FabLearn Conference, Stanford University, September 26–27.

Santamaria, Lorri J. 2009. "Culturally Responsive Differentiated Instruction: Narrowing Gaps between Best Pedagogical Practices Benefiting All Learners." *Teachers College Record* 111 (1): 214–247.

Schmid, Christina. 2017. "An Archive of the Future: Iyapo Repository." *Art-Pulse*, October 25. http://artpulsemagazine.com/an-archive-of-the-future-iya po-repository.

Schultz, Megan. 2011. "Performing Graffiti: The Use of Electronically and Digitally Modified Graffiti in Activist Art Practices." Master's thesis, University of New Mexico.

Schwartz, Lisa, and Kris Gutiérrez. 2015. "Literacy Studies and Situated Methods: Exploring the Social Organization of Household Activity and Family Media Use." In *The Routledge Handbook of Literacy Studies*, edited by Kate Pahl and Jennifer Rowsell, 574–592. New York: Routledge.

Scott, Kimberly A., Kimberly M. Sheridan, and Kevin Clark. 2014. "Culturally Responsive Computing: A Theory Revisited." *Learning, Media and Technology* 40 (4): 412–436.

Sharp, Janet, and Anthony Stevens. 2007. "Culturally-Relevant Algebra Teaching: The Case of African Drumming." *Journal of Mathematics and Culture* 2 (1): 37–57.

Sheared, Vanessa. 1996. "Community Development and Education for Social Change." *Adult Learning* 7 (6): 20–20.

Sheared, Vanessa, and Peggy A. Sissel. 2001. *Making Space: Merging Theory and Practice in Adult Education*. Westport, CT: Greenwood.

Smith, Shaunna, and Danah Henriksen. 2016. "Fail Again, Fail Better: Embracing Failure as a Paradigm for Creative Learning in the Arts." *Art Education* 69 (2): 6–11.

Smitherman, Geneva. 1977. *Talkin and Testifyin: The Language of Black America*. Detroit, MI: Wayne State University Press.

Smitherman, Geneva. 2000. "Ebonics, King, and Oakland: Some Folks Don't Believe Fat Meat Is Greasy." In *Talkin That Talk: Language, Culture and Education in African America*, edited by G. Smitherman, 150–162. New York: Routledge.

Snead, James A. 1990. "Repetition as a Figure of Black Culture." In *Out There: Marginalization and Contemporary Cultures*, edited by Russell Ferguson, 213–232. Cambridge, MA: MIT Press.

Stiny, George, and James Gips. 1972. "Shape Grammars and the Generative Specification of Painting and Sculpture." In *Proceedings of IFIP Congress 1971*, vol. 2, edited by Charles V. Freiman, John E. Griffith, and Jack L. Rosenfeld, 1460–1465. Amsterdam: North Holland Publishing.

Thórisson, Kristinn R., Hrvoje Benko, Denis Abramov, Andrew Arnold, Sameer Maskey, and Aruchunan Vaseekaran. 2004. "Constructionist Design Methodology for Interactive Intelligences." *AI Magazine* 25 (4): 77–90.

Tissenbaum, Mike, Josh Sheldon, and Hal Abelson. 2019. "From Computational Thinking to Computational Action." *Communications of the ACM* 62 (3): 34–36.

Tucker-Raymond, Eli, Brian Gravel, Aditi Wagh, and Naeem Wilson. 2016. "Making It Social: Considering the Purpose of Literacy to Support

Participation in Making and Engineering." *Journal of Adolescent & Adult Literacy* 60 (2): 207–211.

Tuckman, Bruce W. 1965. "Developmental Sequence in Small Groups." *Psychological Bulletin* 63 (6): 384–399.

Turkle, Sherry, and Seymour Papert. 1992. "Epistemological Pluralism and the Revaluation of the Concrete." *Journal of Mathematical Behavior* 11 (1): 3–33.

Vakil, Sepehr, and Rick Ayers. 2019. The Racial Politics of STEM Education in the USA: Interrogations and Explorations. *Race Ethnicity and Education* 22 (4): 449–458.

Veal, Michael. 2007. *Dub: Soundscapes and Shattered Songs in Jamaican Reggae*. Middletown, CT: Wesleyan University Press.

Villarreal, Ignacio. 2014. "Ai Weiwei and Bert Benally Create Pull of the Moon through an Unprecedented International Art Collaboration." *Art Daily*, June 28.

Vineyard, Jennifer. 2014. "How Grandmaster Flash's 'Torque Theory' Drove Hip-Hop." *Vulture*, March 27. https://www.vulture.com/2014/03 /grandmaster-flash-torque-theory-hip-hop.html.

Vossoughi, Shirin, Paula K. Hooper, and Meg Escudé. 2016. "Making through the Lens of Culture and Power: Toward Transformative Visions for Educational Equity." *Harvard Educational Review* 86 (2): 206–232.

Wahlman, Maude S. 2001. *Signs and Symbols: African Images in African-American Quilts*. New York: Museum of American Folk Art.

Wasef, Basem. 2007. *Legendary Motorcycles*. Minneapolis, MN: Motorbooks.

Watkins, Samuel Craig. 2008. *Hip Hop Matters: Politics, Pop Culture, and the Struggle for the Soul of a Movement*. Boston: Beacon Press.

Weber, Jasmine. 2018. "An Afrofeminist Project Uses Technology to Empower Marginalized Communities." *Hyperallergic*, September 18. https:// hyperallergic.com/460424/hyphen-labs.

Wegener, Charlotte, and Marie K. Aakjær. 2016. "Upcycling—a New Perspective on Waste in Social Innovation." *Journal of Comparative Social Work* 11 (2).

Weheliye, Alexander G. 2005. *Phonographies: Grooves in Sonic Afro-modernity*. Durham, NC: Duke University Press.

Williams, Ben. 2002. "The Remixmasters: A History Lesson for Puffy Combs." *Slate Magazine*, July 29. https://slate.com/culture/2002/07/a-history-lesson -for-puffy-combs.html.

Williams, Robin. 2014. *The Non-designers Design Book*. San Francisco, CA: Peachpit Press.

Wing, Jeannette. 2016. "Computational Thinking, 10 Years Later." *Microsoft Research Blog*, March 23. https://www.microsoft.com/en-us/research /blog/computational-thinking-10-years-later.

Winger-Bearskin, Amelia. 2018. "Before Everyone Was Talking about Decentralization, Decentralization Was Talking to Everyone." *Immerse*, July 2. https://immerse.news/decentralized-storytelling-d8450490b3ee.

Wolfe, Maynard Frank. 2000. *Rube Goldberg: Inventions*. New York: Simon & Schuster.

Woloshyn, Alexa. 2015. "Hearing Urban Indigeneity in Canada: Self-Determination, Community Formation, and Kinaesthetic Listening with A Tribe Called Red." *American Indian Culture and Research Journal* 39 (3): 1–23.

Wood, Sherri. 2015. *The Improv Handbook for Modern Quilters: A Guide to Creating, Quilting & Living Courageously*. New York: Stewart, Tabori, & Chang.

Wynter, Sylvia. 1992. "Rethinking 'Aesthetics': Notes towards a Deciphering Practice." In *Exiles: Essays on Caribbean Cinema*, edited by Mbye Cham, 237–279. Trenton, NJ: Africa World Press.

Ybarra-Frausto, Tomás. 2011. "Post-Movimiento: The Contemporary (Re) Generation of Chicana/o Art." In *A Companion to Latina/o Studies*, 289–296. Malden, MA: Wiley-Blackwell.

Ybarra-Frausto, Tomás. 2019. "Rasquachismo: A Chicano Sensibility." In *Chicano and Chicana Art: A Critical Anthology*, 85–90. Durham, NC: Duke University Press.

Zittoun, Tania, and Svend Brinkmann. 2012. "Learning as Meaning Making." In *Encyclopedia of the Sciences of Learning*, edited by Norbert M. Seel. Boston: Springer.

Index

Page numbers in italics indicate a figure on the corresponding page.